Dreams & Destiny

SUNRISE
—BOOKS—

Published by Sunrise Books,
an imprint of
Marshall Cavendish Books Limited
58 Old Compton Street
London W1V 5PA

© Marshall Cavendish Limited 1987
Reprinted 1988

ISBN 0 86307 801 X

Printed and bound in Spain

Credits
Christ Barker pp. 73, 83, 107, 108, 109, 110-11, 113. Steve Bicknell p. 92. The Bodleian Library, Oxford pp. 49, 67, 90, 91. The British Museum, London p. 90. Larry Burrows/Aspect p. 55. Roger Charity p. 17. Salvador Dali p. 60. Alan Duns pp. 80-81. Mary Evans Picture Library pp. 65, 87, 119. John Fernley pp. 25, 52. Fox-Rank p. 61. John Garrett pp. 8, 16, 18, 26, 31. Oslo Kommunes Kunstsamlinger p. 59. The Mansell Collection pp. 52, 53. M.G.M./C.I.C. p. 61. Popperfoto pp. 25, 52. F. Jurgen Rogner pp. 7, 12-13. Sanders p. 33. Kim Sayer p. 63. Malcolm Scoular pp. 84, 95, 103, 120. John Seymour p. 4. Snark International p. 66. Trevor Sutton p. 6. The Tate Gallery, London pp. 10, 21, 40. Victoria and Albert Museum/Crown copyright p. 45. Michael James Ward p. 72. John Watney p. 43. Chris Yates pp. 5, 15, 22, 29, 36, 39, 51, 57, 62. ZEFA/Pictor Ltd p. 35.
Illustrations by Maggie Raynor.
Artwork makeup by Roy Flooks.

Contents

Introduction

Beyond experiencing awareness in our everyday lives, each of us knows another level of reality – the reality of the inner self. Though we may not fully recognize it, our instincts, emotions, thoughts, and judgements of the outside world operate at this level, continuing to occupy our minds even when we are not entirely conscious. It is in sleep, in fact, that we gain access to our inner self, for our dreams can reveal, most vividly, the submerged layers of the mind. For many people dreams are entertaining, intriguing stories and a source of fun. Yet they can be much more. They are recognized as playing an important role in analysis of the mind, and, like well-known devices for predicting the future – such as cards and fortune charts – they can be regarded as indicators of our personal destiny. This book explores both the complex world of dreams, and the wide field of beliefs and methods designed to open the door to the sub-conscious, and possibly even to the paranormal and the future.

Dreams have always been a source of fascination. Early civilizations often set great store by the messages that dreams conveyed. The ancient Babylonians believed that dreams were almost like spells cast by evil spirits, while, much later, the Greeks and Romans became pre-occupied with the symbolic language of sleep. Today we can appreciate the significance of dreams by learning about the work of psychologists such as Freud, Jung and Adler. They explored the meanings of symbols and images seen during sleep, revealing them to be universal, and experienced by the people of all cultures. As the book shows, many early ideas about dreams were not dissimilar to our modern approach to dream analysis. Ancient Chinese thinking, which distinguishes between different levels of consciousness, and Indian beliefs which view series of dreams as capable of resolving problems, have links with the contemporary thought of scientists like Christopher Evans; this scientist, in describing the therapeutic value of dreams, compares our unconscious minds to computers, which uncoupled from the outside world, busily shift information while we sleep.

Yet as this book shows, dreams also find their expression in creative activity. Visions and images seen during sleep are mirrored in our films, paintings and literature, as the poetry of Wordsworth, the art of the Surrealists, and the films of directors such as Luis Bunuel and Alain Resnais illustrate.

While we can explore our inner self by reflecting upon our dreams, there is also the possibility of delving into the sub-conscious and encouraging fate to reveal itself, by experimenting with various fortune-telling devices. The second half of this book therefore, looks at the symbolism of omens, oracles and signs, and explains how we can snatch glimpses of our fate and fortunes by understanding the significance of spilt salt and moles and itches; and by reading 'random' patterns – whether they occur as swirling tea-leaves, or as thrown dice, or shuffled dominoes.

The ancient practices of palmistry and numerology, together with the more recent theory of phrenology, are explained in detail, and throughout there is sound advice about interpreting what is revealed. In conclusion the book explores the most aristocratic of oracles, the Tarot cards and the I Ching, or the Chinese Book of Changes – two paths to prophecy, which like dreams, may be regarded as routes towards our inner selves.

Dream for yourself

Most people think that dreams are some kind of night-time joke. How often has a friend come over at work or in the shops and said, 'I had the oddest, funniest dream last night'? This is usually the start of a good story, usually a jumble of strange ideas perhaps involving a mutual friend, set in the most unlikely circumstances or filled with such terror and fear that no one can understand the reason for it. The normal reaction is to marvel at the oddity of it all—and then forget about it. But you can get much more out of dreams than jokes or strange stories. It is interesting to note for instance that people always want to tell their dream

to someone, as if there is a natural desire to go back over the experience, to try and think it out. With a little knowledge and experience you'll be able to learn some valuable things about yourself and your friends— about character, aims, ambitions and the problems which are bothering your unconscious. You might even find a solution to a dilemma which has been worrying you for days.

The most important step is to realize that dreams are not disorganized nonsense. Your brain isn't resting by

Night-time experiences can seem as vivid as waking reality.

CHRIS YATES

5

F JÜRGEN ROGNER

Dreams have their own logic – a car can be the driving force in your life; (right) falling can suggest a sense of losing a grip on life.

scrambling up thoughts and turning everything upside-down for a few hours while your body relaxes. Neither are dreams some frightening glimpse into the 'dark world' of the mind. There is nothing dangerous or harmful about dwelling on your dreams, though

you don't need to be obsessive about it.

Psychology and dreams

Many people think that all the talk about 'the mind' and 'psychoanalysis' involved in dream interpretation is nonsense. But you should not make the mistake of thinking it is a pseudo-science, fit only for ridicule. The work of famous psychoanalysts like Freud and Jung has helped thousands of normal, healthy people, to say nothing

of many cases of extreme mental disturbance. Their findings can be applied in a simple way to everyone's own experience of life. You don't have to be neurotic, obsessive or anything else so serious. Just as doctors can treat grave physical diseases but also show the world in general the basic rules of personal or home hygiene, so psychologists have shown well-balanced human beings how they can be more self-aware and lead, fuller happier lives.

7

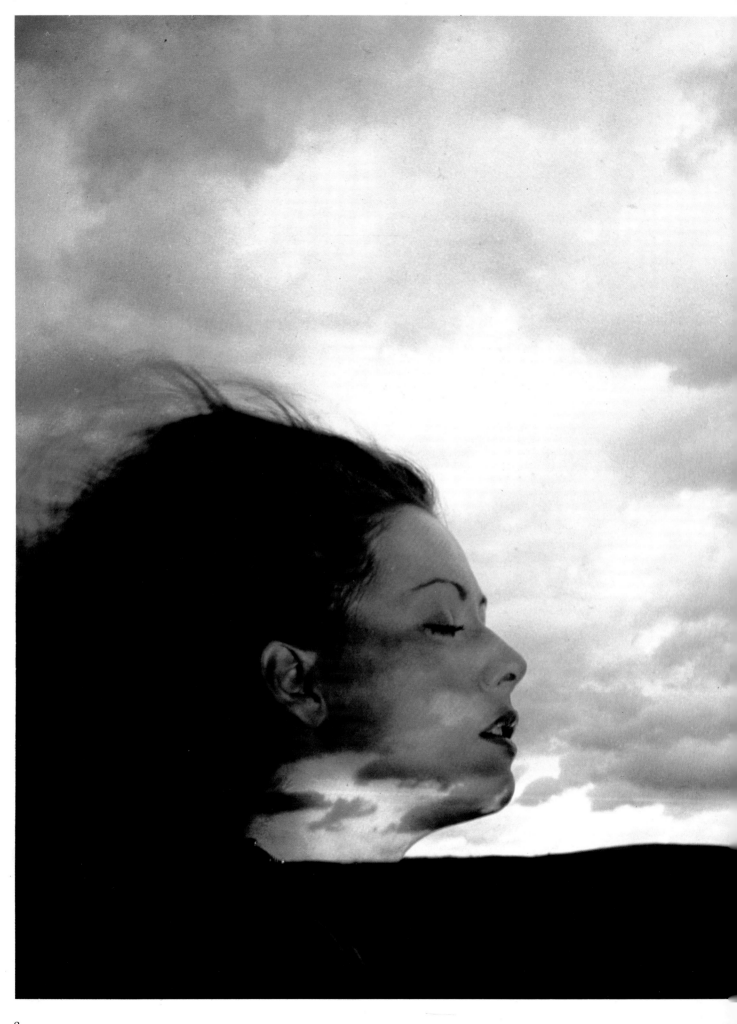

What are dreams?

What are dreams exactly? There are many theories about the meaning of dreams but everyone basically agrees that they are a product of the unconscious mind. This is best explained by looking at what happens when people daydream. The mind is wide-awake and aware—that is, conscious. You might be going out shopping, knitting or filing cards in a perfectly ordinary way, but your thoughts wander on their own. Perhaps you go over what happened last night, or more often, what you hope will happen in the future. Sometimes these daydreams become quite divorced from reality; people imagine themselves on Caribbean beaches or married to millionaires. While it lasts, a daydream seems vivid and true, but when you 'snap out of it' it is easy to forget. Something of the same process occurs in dreams which take place during sleep. The conscious, controlling part of the mind becomes relaxed (although it does not switch off all its powers) and a submerged layer of thoughts, ideas and feelings wells up. Because this part of the mind obeys its own logic, it describes things in its own direct way, using word-pictures and seemingly irrational chains of connections. This is why in dreams people do impossible things or shift quickly from scene to scene. The unconscious mind is going direct to the point without needing to progress in a logical sequence as the conscious mind does.

The other characteristic of dreams, which everyone who recalls them will recognize, is that they are often unusually vivid—either visually or in mood. Sometimes the feelings they generate can be so strong that they affect the dreamer's mood for the next day—sometimes called 'getting out of bed on the wrong side'. For instance, a successful businessman related a series of dreams he had during the early part of his career, all of which were set in a war situation. (War is one of the classic images of pressure or tension.) At first, while he was working on his own, his dreams involved his own attempts to avoid some nameless terror which came in a variety of guises. After he took control of a large department in a big company the war dreams continued, except his main preoccupation became trying to get the other people in the dream to cope with the attack, or whatever it happened to be. Significantly he could not recall the visual detail of the dreams—apart from the wartime setting—but the feelings of fear, panic and frustration associated with them re-mained particularly vivid.

On the good side, it is quite common to have a very happy or successful dream and to wake up feeling particularly pleased with yourself. Small children for example often dream of receiving gifts: they wake up feeling curiously elated and can be very down-hearted when they realize it was only a dream! Typical is the story of a small boy who was telling his mother in great excitement about his dream of the night before. He was being chased by a wolf and had tried to run into the house for protection through the kitchen door, but it would not open. He struggled and struggled as the fierce wolf drew nearer, then finally at the last minute, the door handle gave and he got inside to safety. The boy's mother replied in the usual way, 'Oh well, never mind, it was only a dream', to which the child retorted, 'Well, next time I have a dream, you leave the door open!' Children have to learn to distinguish between the 'inner space' of the unconscious and the 'outer space' of consciousness. Some primitive tribes still make no differentiation between the two.

This 'alternative reality' of dreams is very important. Allied to it is the fact that dreams happen entirely of their own accord, and we cannot make them happen or control their contents.

What dreams do

What are dreams for? Basically, they are the method by which the unconscious mind sifts and sorts experiences. If you can visualize the brain as an enormous receiving station, with all kinds of information going into it every day, then you will see that it has a large task to perform. During sleep, while the conscious part of the mind is inactive, the unconscious, (or subconscious) processes a vast jumble of material—new facts, situations, past experiences, unsolved worries, fears, desires and much more. It draws up emotions from the deepest recesses of the mind and memory and takes into account all the new information which the conscious mind has received. Then, in its own unique style, it presents a visual and emotional image to you—a dream. Perhaps you have a problem which you are consciously putting off because you do not wish to think about it. But it is still there and may well present itself to you in a dream. The sorting station is sending a message, 'Don't forget, don't overlook this'. Sometimes a dream will even offer a possible solution to such a problem.

As well as the unconscious, there is that deeper part already mentioned where the instincts, intuitions and emotions originate. These too are drawn up into dreams through the sorting house function, producing a very powerful effect on the mind. Just as people push problems to one side consciously, so also they ignore real feelings. It is interesting to note that people often say, 'What do you think about So-and-so, really, deep down?' or 'In my heart of hearts I believe such-and-such', as if in common speech they acknowledge the existence of this innermost part of the mind where strong, genuine feelings are to be found.

By recognizing where the material that goes into dreams comes from, you can begin to understand more of your true nature—your real views and attitudes, your feelings and needs, and by relating the dream-pictures to your everyday existence, get a better grip on your life-situation. Not all dreams are exactly problem-posers or -solvers, but they are a representation of some part of your life, often that part with which you cope least successfully.

> 'I dreamed I was dying in a lonely room. This funny doctor was there but no-one else. The doctor said there was nothing he could do but I was going to die. I wasn't in any pain — it wasn't a nightmare. I didn't really remember it until going to the office next morning. I kept thinking about it all day.'
> Businesswoman, 29

People who don't dream

What about people who say they never dream? If thinking about dreams is so helpful, why do some people never recall them—are they missing out in some way? Most of them are perfectly happy, average human beings, with no apparent disadvantage in comparison with those who seem to dream regularly. Laboratory experiments using the electro-encephalograph (EEG) machine to record brain 'waves' have revealed that people who do not recall their dreams have exactly the same trace patterns as those who remember their dreams vividly. In fact everyone dreams for regular periods during the night and people who think they never dream either forget them or have 'thoughts' in the night which they do not consider to be dreams—more like daydreams. If you are one of these 'non-recallers' try discussing dreams with people who do remember them. You will probably find that you begin to recall them more often.

What dreams can tell you

For those who can remember dreams, the next step is to uncover the real meaning behind them. The key to the subject is that dreams are what a famous American psychologist Calvin Hall once termed 'a letter to oneself'. Once you have learned to read this private letter, some fascinating home truths will emerge. Do not believe that dreams will necessarily show you the answers to all your problems—no dream ever repaired a damaged bank balance or turned an ugly duckling into a swan! But it might help you to see that money is not all-important and that a good face or figure is not the be-all and end-all of life.

The best way to start examining your dreams is simply to recall them during the following day. Just mulling them over, even if they seem quite non-sensical, will be of help. Sometimes a thought will suddenly spring into your mind as a result of these ponderings. It might appear at first to have no connection whatsoever with the dream, but a little more thought will reveal the link. For example, it often happens that a friend introduces you to someone about whom you have heard a great deal of praise and glory. You feel a small prick of doubt, but immediately dismiss it and try to socialize. In the end, you come to the conclusion that this new individual is 'not so bad' after all. It is possible that you will have a dream after such an encounter in which this charming and apparently successful person is turned into a ridiculous figure, a hideous monster or a creepy-crawly insect—depending on the nature of your real view. That first 'suppressed' reaction will come back in dream form, and conversely, dwelling on the dream could bring back the reaction.

Recording your dreams

Another way in which dreams can inform the dreamer is if they are studied over a period of time. Keep a notebook, writing down each dream either at night if you wake up from a particularly disturbing one (which will also help you to return to calm sleep) or first thing in the morning before getting up. Do not simply make a note of the basic situation of the dream—like 'Climbed mountain'—but try to catch in a word or two the essential feeling involved: 'Climbed mountain, made great effort, seemed to take a long time, but felt very pleased when top reached'. It is also very important to follow the sequence of events as they occur in the dream. You often find that you do things for reasons which, in waking life, you might think were totally

Below: Richard Hamilton's 'Interior II' conveys in pop art terms the theory that dream images are all reflections of the dreamer's personality. You can evaluate the significance of each image separately —combined together they will form a coherent expression of your inner state. The objects in this painting are familiar but fragmented; in the same way, dream images are drawn from everyday objects but are presented in stark juxtaposition.

irrelevant or illogical. Next time you tell a dream to a friend note how often you say 'I did such-and-such *because*'. This feeling of compulsion is often very strong during dreams. Take the following example: 'I was running down a narrow dead-end street because a huge tank was bearing down on me.' The chain of events is part of the dream's private language—its message to you. Suppose the tank represents a person's sense of ambition. Perhaps the dream means that if the ambition is followed single-mindedly, without other possibilities being taken into account, it might be a mistake, for it will lead into a dead-end situation. The dream gives a clue to help you work out its contents by the order in which events are presented.

Dreaming in series

Similarly, series of dreams can be especially revealing. Although the dreamer may see himself very differently in each isolated dream, if they are put into a sequence, a pattern will emerge, revealing at least the area of his preoccupation.

Sometimes a series of dreams will show a progression in thinking. If you have some underlying conflict, such as an inability to get along with a relative, a series of dreams may play out numerous alternatives, like being very aggressive or being loving and submissive, or even murderous in hatred. What is difficult to recognize in one dream may be more easily seen when two or three dreams are put together to look for common features.

This serial aspect may seem difficult at first. Take the two dreams described here:

'I was going to a big, strange house in the country which my family had just moved into — but it was empty. I was being driven there in a car in my night clothes, all wrapped up in a blanket in the front passenger seat, but there was no one in the driver's seat. Suddenly I was there — I don't remember arriving — and I went up to a room where there was a man putting up wallpaper. It was incredible wallpaper, in three parts. The first part was a collage of sparkly Christmas cards. The second was a boat — a galleon made out of gold paper — and the third part had a Teddy bear stuck on to it. It was about 2 feet high, and in a running position, stuck on sideways. I was talking to the decorator. I can't remember exactly what I said, but it was something about how much work must have gone into it, and the decorator was going on about how wonderful it was. Then suddenly I was dressed in my day clothes. Sue, a friend of mine, came in dressed in a funny coat and said, "Today's my day for learning". (I knew it was Tuesday, even outside my dream, and she goes to college on Tuesdays). Then I found a piece of paper which said "Please phone Clive before 19.19". Then the phone rang and I woke up and Clive was on the other end.'

'I was in this travelling show and there were many players but I was with the guy who owned the show and I looked like one of those "Barbie" dolls...you know... those "Cindy" dolls . . . and not looking at all human. I did all these astounding things which only a doll could do and which a human would hurt herself doing. At the end of the show I had a metal comb which I had to hold in my mouth and make it go round so it made my mouth bleed . . . the whole of the inside of my mouth was bleeding. I had to put my finger in my mouth and hold it up to the audience to show the blood to prove I was really human!'

There are certain elements common to both these dreams, even though at first glance they appear very different. For a start, there is a feeling of passivity around the dreamer in both cases: in the first dream she is being driven—as opposed to driving the car herself—and is all wrapped up, motionless, powerless, like a little child or baby. This ties in with the second dream's idea of being like a 'doll', that takes orders from a boss-man. Secondly, both dreams are connected with children. The doll is an object associated with childhood. In the first dream, the girl enters a room that sounds like a fantastic nursery, with pretty Christmas cards and Teddy Bear wallpaper. The dreamer herself could probably add greater meaning to this part of the dream by looking in her memory for incidents connected with boats, Teddy bears and Christmas. In general terms, these pictures suggest she is looking back into her childhood as a time when everything was done for her, with a 'lot of work going into it' as she says in the dream.

Obviously, connections with childhood in the second dream are the doll, but in the main it is concerned with the present. The girl is on her own and somehow associated with a man who makes her do terrible tricks. It does not take a great deal of analytical skill to start wondering whether in real life this dreamer is mixed up with someone who is or has made her hide her real feelings and has hurt her. It might even be a more general situation: the girl might be afraid of having any relationship with a man at all. Only she can tell. Yet, even you as an outsider can progress quite far with this series of dreams. You can see clearly how the same problem-area is covered in both. Here is a girl, who remembers a comfortable happy time at home, now confronted with a new way of living and

'I walk through the stage door of a huge theatre and then discover that to get on to the stage itself, I have to walk down a really enormous, long, but wide, flight of stairs. It is almost like a ladder — there is no rail or handhold — but the steps are flat like a staircase. I am terrified of heights, have always been, but I manage to make it all the way to the bottom without falling. Then, I discover that I'm in a huge complex of caves and one is so small that I'm afraid to go through it for fear I won't be able to get back again.'
Copy editor, 31, female

relating to people, on her own and feeling apprehensive, even hurt, by her new experiences. The first dream moves on further from the happy childhood picture: there is another girl in it saying 'Today's my day for learning.' The message for the dreamer is 'Buck up and don't look back, let's get on with living, however difficult it is'. This links up quite specifically with the end of the other dream. The outside stimulus of the telephone ringing brings to mind the subject area of the problem, that is, dealing with men on an adult level. Comfortingly, the dream is urging her with a 'message' to make contact: 'Go on, give it a try'. The second dream about the doll sticks to the same situation but expresses the girl's fears about the possible outcome —being used and hurt. Incidentally, the dreamer was astonished at the accuracy of the insights in this inter-

Above: Images can be drawn from any time in your past. They could be zebras from a childhood visit to the zoo combined with last week's holiday flight. These images in turn might be expressed in the style of some science fiction film you saw the evening before.

pretation, which was made without any background information.

No time in dreams

Another aspect of this link-up in dreams of different kinds of pictures is that the dreaming mind takes no notice whatsoever of time, which is part of the conscious mind's experience: it simply doesn't need it. In a dream, something that happened to you ten years ago may be relevant to something that is part of your life today. Look for

F. JÜRGEN ROGNER

very helpful. To use the examples just discussed: if the girl's recollection of childhood was of a time when she was very unhappy and lonely, then obviously the dream would have a different message. The series might be saying 'You'll be hurt again just as you were before, so be careful'. Either way, the problem is a common one, that of reconciling the past with the present and growing up.

How to recall your dreams

For those people who seldom or never recall a dream and feel a little frustrated at the prospect of missing out in this personal 'fortune-telling', some comfort can be derived from the fact that telling yourself 'I'll have a dream tonight' can sometimes produce interesting results. Ann Faraday, a well-known British dream researcher, has formulated some rules to help people catch their dreams. She recommends setting an alarm clock to go off at two-hourly intervals from the usual falling-asleep time. In this way, you can be fairly sure of catching yourself during a dreaming patch. Even a once-nightly interruption will do, if the idea of more sounds like torture, but in this case, set the clock for much later in the night—between 3 and 5 am.

If you do wake up this way, it is essential to write the dream details down then and there or they will fade very quickly. Better still, use a cassette tape recorder if you have one, and keep it by the bedside. Failing that, tell it to your sleeping partner or say it out loud—this helps to get the details up into the conscious mind which then stores it in the recent memory.

At whatever time you awake with a dream whether in the night or in the morning, it is advisable to move slowly —do not jar yourself into reality if you want to catch the most details possible. Leaping out of bed to rush across the room for a pencil will probably result in your stopping dead in your tracks with a sudden blank in your mind. Move gently, slowly, into a sitting position— some people find it helpful to keep their eyes closed for a few moments while they capture as many details as they can. The small things in a dream can frequently be significant, as for example in making a serial record over a period of time. Perhaps a small detail in one dream may become the central part of another, or a picture with a similar connotation may appear subsequently. Either way, it is important to lose as little as possible so you can have plenty of material to ponder over.

common links in events, and do not concentrate on writing down only those dreams which seem to be the most coherent or the most like waking views of life.

It follows from this that if a picture or incident in a dream reminds you

immediately of something in your past, you must note it down as well. Psychoanalysts have found that one of the most useful interpretations of a dream is that made by the patient himself. So even in studying your dreams in a nonclinical way, such connections will be

Analysis: nine dreams

If you could ask one hundred people what they thought was the mood conveyed in their dreams, about forty would probably answer that it was apprehension. About eighteen would say anger, then perhaps six would mention sadness. Only a lucky eighteen individuals would be able to state that happiness was the main emotional content of their dreams. The remaining eighteen would describe sensations of surprise, excitement or interest.

These figures were established in a very wide-reaching survey conducted in the early 1950s, just fifty years after the first publication of *The Interpretation of Dreams* by Sigmund Freud. In that space of time the issues he first investigated have been confirmed and modified. Nowadays we have a fairly clear picture of the sort of things people dream about. The following samples are typical of normal sleep experiences.

Sex on a desert island

Freud's great contribution to the understanding of dreams was his realization that they reflect unconscious thought processes, especially with regard to sexual drives. Sex can be presented directly, as in dreams which actually involve making love. More often the sexual message is hidden in some way. This is especially true where the dreamer has some sense of guilt or conflict between his desire and his conscience.

'I dreamt I was on a beautiful desert island, green parrots were flying overhead, and suddenly Marlon Brando appeared. I was wearing a very brightly patterned sarong thing, and he said I looked like a flower . . . the next thing we're sitting in a beautiful clearing in a thick shady forest, and there's a mass of fruit and food piled up for our picnic . . . the rest of the dream was all about . . . well, making love.'

The setting
This is a classic example of a sexual dream in more ways than the obvious ending. 'A beautiful desert island' is an exotic, faraway-from-it-all setting. Sex is often suggested in such lush or luxuriously different places. It is essential to notice the background setting of any dreams. Domestic, familiar places occur most frequently. Places of pleasure or sport, such as football grounds or swimming pools, are almost as common, whereas work places are much less frequent, in spite of the amount of time spent there in waking life.

The setting or background can reveal something about the meaning of a dream when evaluated in relation to the events taking place there. Here, clearly, the desert island reinforces the out-of-the-ordinary character of the dream and suggests that it is pure wish-fulfilment.

The hero
A glamorous film star like Marlon Brando may be part of the same desire for romance and sexual excitement. It is quite common to dream of famous people, colleagues from work or social acquaintances (like other people's husbands or wives) in this situation. It does not necessarily mean that you want to make love to that person in reality. You might simply be linking up a wish for sexual satisfaction with an example of the sort of person you like. Consider the character of the film star or friend in the dream, for it may give you some insight into the qualities you admire in a partner in real life. It is perfectly normal for a married person to dream about distant individuals in preference to real lovers or spouses. If your actual relationship is satisfactory then you will probably not reflect upon it often in a dream, which is usually a time for satisfying unmet desires or sorting out problem situations.

The role of the dreamer
In a dream such as this, you should also look at how you place yourself. Is the 'I' figure really like you? Do you find it laughable to think of yourself dressed in bright colours or hearing pretty compliments? Perhaps you think you are not very attractive or that your personality lacks real colour. Your dream may be compensating for these feelings. How do you respond to the idea of all that food? Do you eat it with appetite and pleasure or just toy with it? Remember that food is often a sexual symbol, representing the idea of appetite for sex as well as for sustenance. This is a good example of the way the sexual message of a dream can be hidden under another subject.

The great escape

According to Alfred Adler, another of the great dream psychologists, the commonest drive besides sex is that for power. Dreams frequently reveal the hidden desires of a personality or release some urges that do not find satisfaction in real life.

'I had a really vivid dream of being with a group of men, we were prisoners in a sort of castle — there were soldiers on guard duty everywhere. I organized the men into an escape group. I seemed to be able to speak several languages, so I was the leader, and we dug a tunnel to get out. Then we were climbing over a very high wall . . . it seemed to take ages. Lastly I remember standing on an open train carriage, and rushing through countryside, feeling excited we'd escaped, but worried in case we were being followed.'

You might have guessed already that this is a man's dream—not that women do not also dream of action and power, but proportionately more men than women are concerned with these issues in dreams. This is a reflection of the differences in physical characteristics and the roles usually assigned to the two sexes in society.

The role of the dreamer
Here, the 'I' in the dream is significant again. Is the dreamer rather timid in real life, working at a job that lacks any outgoing action? If this were true, then the dream would be compensatory—making up for the lack he feels in his situation. It might also be an expression

Right: Doorways, staircases, castles, churches—however remote from everyday experience—are common dream images because of their general emotive value.

14

Jungians believe that everything in a dream is a reflection of some part of yourself, so being alone in a bare room might suggest a need to look inward. A Freudian interpretation might give this image a sexual connotation.

of a man's need to dominate, to organize, to be brave and tough. Alfred Adler, who started out as a disciple of Freud but subsequently developed his own views, placed a lot of emphasis on this aggressive drive in people, believing it was as important as sex.

The influence of recent experience
Such a dream might be prompted by watching a Western or wartime adventure at the movies or on television. However, it is important not to overestimate the 'trigger' of a dream as its cause. The recent experience might produce the particular situation of the dream, but it has nothing more to do with why that particular event—of all others in the recent past—should be retained and re-created in the dream.

Private doubts and fears
A very large proportion of dreams dwell on feelings of doubt, fear or inadequacy. There is a trace of that in this dream, for the escaped man is still worried that he is being followed. In other words, even after he has shown himself to be brave and resourceful, he thinks that it is still not enough and he hurries away on the train to the next challenge. This dreamer probably pushes himself too hard and should learn to accept his limitations. He might not appear like this at all in real life. It is surprising what doubts are expressed in this private way.

Black cats in the basement

'I went into a tall house, down a dark staircase. I don't know why I was there but I seemed to know which way to go. I got into a dark room, it seemed empty, then suddenly I realized it was seething with cats. Black cats. Then I realized that I had a baby in a kind of papoose, strapped to my back. I turned to get out of the room, and a cat jumped on my back and was clinging on to the baby. I tried to get out of the house and was running along trying to get the cat off my back all the time.'

Animals and instincts
Such a dream leads inevitably to an analysis of images and symbols in dreams. What do the pictures suggest to the dreamer? There are two main levels of interpretation here. Take the cats first. By and large animals represent the instincts, the emotional, intuitive parts of a person's nature as opposed to the rational, controlling parts. But it is also significant to find

out what the dreamer actually thinks of the animals in her dream, in this case black cats. If for example the person had a favourite pet that died, there might be a strong sense of loving and deep loss associated with cats in her mind. By contrast, the girl who related this dream had always rather disliked them. Their feline movements were too 'creepy-crawly' for her, and she did not like the suddenness with which they bare their claws. This relates back to the general symbolic values associated with them: intuitive, instinctive, especially female emotions. Notice how this is linked in the dream with the picture of the baby tied to the girl's back. A fear of her own feelings is being expressed.

The setting
The setting of the dream as always yields some meaning too. Houses occur frequently in dreams. Living rooms, bedrooms and kitchens turn up most, in that order. Basements and cellars are places where 'base' deeds are committed, where deep feelings are allowed out. The dream seems to suggest not only a fear of discovering deep-hidden feelings, but a hint of the anxiety or hurt that could result from giving way to them.

Different parts of the whole
It is worthwhile analyzing a dream as if everything in it, including people, is a part of the dreamer.

This house stands for the girl herself: the cellar, her own instinctive feelings; the baby may not mean another human being or a desire for children, but a part of the girl herself that she is afraid to express. She is afraid of getting hurt if she does. Obviously, the dreamer herself can tell best to what the images refer. This dream does not answer the questions, but poses them. Somewhere in her unconscious there are deep feelings trying to be expressed.

The turquoise pool

Other dreams work through a problem to a solution. Most of us have had a dream at some point which is repeated, perhaps even over a span of several years. These are known as 'recurring' dreams. Quite often they relate back to some incident in childhood, if you think

The cat is a familiar image of mystery, associated with magic or religion. In general terms, it represents the intuitive, instinctive, feminine qualities.

closely about it. These dreams are often nightmares and it is the old, familiar quality of only half understanding that is especially frightening.

'I dreamt I fell into a lovely turquoise pool — a beautiful blue, with sponges and ferns floating in the water, growing down the sides of the rocks. At first it looked very pretty and I swam about. Then I realized that it was getting darker, deeper, and I was going down . . . I couldn't breathe, I struggled to come up, and I woke up trying to gasp and take in air.'

Re-living the birth trauma
The endurance of an experience from childhood or birth is partly due to the extreme vividness of the incident in a child's mind and partly results from any reinforcement in later life. This dream is typical of 'drowning' dreams which have been explained by Freud as a lingering remembrance of the birth experience or 'trauma', the uterine waters and the journey from the womb, just as he interpreted 'flying' dreams as a manifestation of sexual ecstacy. If later life brings a sense of insecurity and fear to add to the original experience, then a fear-expressing dream on the same theme may result.

Resolving childhood experiences
Sometimes nightmares refer not to birth experiences but to some childhood incident not resolved or coped with at the time. Even a memory of learning to swim or slipping in the bath might be so vivid that a repeating nightmare remains. Dreams can then be helpful: they go over an incident many times but modify the experience until the difficulty is resolved.
In this case, a child had been playing near a pool and had overheard someone remark on its depth. Her dream was a realization of what might have happened if she had slipped—acting as a very vivid warning.

The collective unconscious
Another theory from the great psychologist and theoretician Carl Gustav Jung suggests that monsters in dreams or other terrifying experiences in nightmares are part of our 'collective unconscious'—a sense of shared experience accumulated over thousands of years of evolution in the unconscious minds of all human beings. These experiences manifest themselves in dreams, always in repeated,'archetypal' ways. Drowning in seas, oceans or lakes is one such motif. (This difficult concept is de-

scribed fully in the section on Jung's theories.)

A legal salad dressing

On the brighter side, a number of delightful dreams seem to satisfy our wildest hopes in improbable ways. Children especially dream in these wish-fulfilling ways because in real life they have little power to do things for themselves. This idea of wish-fulfilment is central to dream interpretation.

'I dreamed I was looking for a job with a firm of lawyers, and I went for an interview to a place. When I got in, one of the partners was mixing up a lovely salad dressing, another was carefully warming glasses for drinks over a roaring fire. The secretary was sorting out beautiful new books — pretty books on all the things I like — crafts, biographies and so on, and putting them on the shelves. I said to myself, "I hope they take me on here, it looks like a good place to work". I felt very happy and decided about it.'

The value of images
Here is a clear case of wishful dreaming, for the girl involved was in real life looking for a job at the time. Why does the dream translate it into such unlikely, incongruous terms? It shows the value of the images of a dream, for all these things—cooking, drinking, reading—are the things that give the dreamer pleasure. Putting them all in one place is like saying 'It's got everything to make me happy'. It could also define a conflict between the job hunting and domestic life. The dreamer, a woman, might secretly be wondering whether she would be better off staying at home. However, the domestic details are highly idealized, with roaring fires and cosy drinks. It suggests that the first analysis is appropriate, merely bringing together images of happiness.

Following the plot
Always follow the sequence of events in a dream: here the conclusion is very significant, for there is a definite decision that getting a good job would be very nice. The dreamer expresses her aim, after a possible conflict.

Parents in the pavilion

Contrasts or comparison between two possible lines of action is the major area of dream experiences. The one above shows a typical problem for a

woman, the choice of taking a job or taking care of her home. Even more fundamental to both sexes is the battle between the desire for freedom and the need for security, especially when growing up and leaving home.

'I'd just got married to someone who in real life is a friend I've known a long time and I'm very close to, but my parents have never met him. The two of us were standing in a huge playing field, like a football ground, and 'way, 'way in the distance inside the pavilion my parents were standing with the rest of my family. We were just about to go off when my parents called, "Haven't you forgotten something?" I thought, "No, I don't think so, I've got enough money etc." They called again, "Haven't you forgotten something?" and again I couldn't think of anything else I needed. They called again, so eventually I relented and we went back all the way over this field to the pavilion where they were standing. When we got there, they said, "We haven't been introduced", so I introduced my "husband" to them and we went off.'

Dreaming about marriage
It is surprising but true that when girls dream about marriage they often put someone they would not expect to marry in the role of bridegroom. This seems to express the general importance and apprehension that women attach to marriage. Men much more normally dream of marriage to girls they do intend to marry in reality. The conflicts inherent in marriage do not seem to strike them to the same degree.

The setting
The choice between family ties and starting a life with a man of her own is expressed here in the image of the football field. The step she had taken means standing out alone in the 'playing field' of life. An element of competition, or striving in the face of the crowd, is suggested. In the pavilion everything is snug and friendly. There is the companionship of the family to be enjoyed. Also, pavilions are places where people relax from the rigours of the game. No one has to bother about the rules of the field.

The spoken words
So in the dream, the conflict is stated and the choice is made, but the dreamer is still not sure. 'Have you forgotten

something?' her parents call. The dreamer could be expressing guilt that she has broken her family ties rather sharply and ought to keep in touch more often. It could be that she still feels that she has to be 'sent off' by her parents, just as a little girl gets dispatched to a party: 'Make sure you're good: have you got a clean handkerchief?' It seems to be that sort of question here. Finally, the dreamer relents and goes back—after the mystical 'three calls', a detail which Jung, with his insistence on religious and folkloric elements would have found very important. The girl makes the introduction—that is, makes the link between her new life and her past—and then goes off.

Problems and solutions

This is a very clear demonstration of the way that dreams not only present a problem or a conflict, but frequently come up with some suggestion for a solution. In real life this girl would probably feel much better about her independence if she matched it with a family contact. It could be that she has always fought hard to stand on her own two feet, whereas in reality she now lacks a little of the kindly assurance that good family ties can give. As with all dream analysis, it is the dreamer herself who must sift the likely explanations and accept the correct, meaningful one.

The woman on the cliff

Perhaps less commonly identified are those dreams which not only offer a solution, but positively inspire the dreamer. Most famous people whose lives have called for tremendous courage in adversity or for a particularly strong sense of ambition can recall dreams where their goal was presented to them in some uplifting way. On a more personal level, we can dream about our better natures, pulling through or surviving a difficult time in life. Jung developed a theory that certain male or female figures in dreams are not necessarily sexual partners, but representatives of the 'opposites' in each person. For a woman, this is her Animus, or male counterpart; for a man, his Anima. These figures can appear in inspirational or guiding roles.

'This dream I had about 12 or 13 years ago but I remember it clearly, it was so vivid. I was in a car being driven along — I was in the passenger seat but I never saw the driver full face, only in profile. We were driving along a coast road with the sea on my side and fields on the driver's side running right down the road with no fence or ditch. The grass was incredibly green. After a while the road began to climb steeply up a cliff, and there was a sheer drop now on my side. On and on, up and up we drove until suddenly the road stopped at the bottom of a sheer crag. At the top stood three figures in dark clothes — two men with a woman between them. I didn't recognize her, though she seemed familiar. I got out of the car to take a closer look. The driver remained seated. I couldn't see any way of getting up the cliff, but then the woman, who was quite good-looking and well-spoken, said to me, "It's not as difficult as it looks. I for one would be most disappointed if you didn't make the effort". Then I started to climb the cliff-face up to her and to my surprise found it wasn't too difficult; as I went, I found handholds and footholds. As I got to the top, the woman leaned down and gave me her hand, helping me up. Then I woke up.'

The search for a goal

This man's dream is disturbingly vivid in its sense of striving and searching for a goal. Hopefully, the dreamer derived some comfort from this vision of a way out of his problems, which in his real life were causing him a great deal of unhappiness.

The car

First, the image of the car stands for a 'journey through life' that contains strongly mechanical or dissatisfying elements. Compare this with dreaming of riding a horse, a natural and exciting method of transport. The suggestion is reinforced by the fact that the dreamer is a passenger, carried through life by a person he doesn't really see properly. Remember that all parts of a dream may be analyzed as reflections of the dreamer himself: this driver is the 'front man' of the dreamer's own personality, not really matching up to his own true sense of himself, but somehow going through the motions of living.

The setting

Dreams are remarkably accurate in the location of an event. Here, the dreamer has the sea on his side. The sea is a symbol of the unconscious, creative forces of the universe and of the 'psyche', or mind. This is the potential area of the man's mind, whereas on his driver's side, there is green grass. You might overlook such a very familiar connection in your own dreams—this image suggests the common phrase 'the grass is always greener on the other side'. Is this the way of life that the dreamer really wants? Is it perhaps just a general discontent that things should be better, more interesting or exciting?

'I went into my parents' house while they were away. I'd just got in through the front door when I sensed that there was someone else in the house. I saw an ultra-enormous man standing in the kitchen with his back to me, sorting through the drawer where all the kitchen knives are kept. I tried to shout but no words came out and I then swivelled round and tried to run out of the house but my feet were completely glued to the floor. I looked over my shoulder to see if he really was still there and saw that he was about to turn round and see me. I then passed out!'
Fashion journalist, 22, female

The climb

The steep climb is a widely-found way of expressing a problem, a difficulty encountered in life. Unfortunately for this man, the endless struggle just leads to more difficulty, until part of him thinks 'I can't go on like this.' This is symbolized by the end of the road at the bottom of the crag.

The three figures

But there are figures at the top of the cliff—the two sides of himself and a kindly encouraging woman, who represents his Anima. For the first time in the dream, the man does something positive. He gets out of the car, leaving his driver behind. The inspirational force leads him to face the challenge of

William Blake's 'Ascent of the Mountain of Purgatory' combines three major dream symbols. The ocean represents the unconscious, the untapped source of creative potential; the climb of the mountain suggests the upward struggle through life, the vision of the woman, a perfect example of the Anima, stands for the inspiration and encouragement to carry on.

Png
Canto 4

his problems and to surmount them. There are footholds in the cliff, just as there are remedies for life's crises.

The will to survive

This dream is a wonderful expression of a man's unconscious will to survive against the odds, to search out his true identity and make a better life for himself. No one can doubt the sincerity of his inner voice, which in a moment of weakness will not permit him to give up. It is not surprising that this man still remembers his moment of truth over a decade later.

A tractor in the living room

The sense of urgency that imbues many dreams demonstrates the power of the mind to force messages up from the unconscious to the surface. Fears, desires, drives or hopes can be expressed in this dream language. Dreams seem to draw our attention to problems or facts consciously overlooked.

'In my dream the living room in my house was extended into a long hall, like a room in a stately palace. The same carpet I've got in real life was laid all down the length of it. What was silly was that some idiot had driven a huge tractor or tank right down this hall and made two great torn-up track marks all down the carpet. A man was lurking about at the end of the room, and I spent most of the dream calling out indignantly, "Who the hell did this?" and trying to get the man to apologize.'

The immediate problem

This dream deals with a most immediate problem. The woman who related it had been dressmaking the night before while watching television and, rather than stand in a cold kitchen, had ironed a few pattern pieces on the floor over a towel. The next day she recalled the dream, but couldn't think what it meant at all. Then, later that same afternoon, her husband noticed a six-inch long stain on the living room carpet. It proved to be a scorch mark where the hot iron had accidentally gone off the towel on to the floor the night before. The woman had not noticed this at all at the time—in fact, it took some minutes for her to realize

Many people have recurrent dreams of their ideal landscape, possibly recalling a happy incident in the past. Distortion of size is often characteristic of childhood memories.

how the mark had been made. Somehow, the incident had registered in her unconscious mind, and her dream had tried to bring it to her attention.

The missing marquee

Dreams can range from the sublime to the ridiculous in their content and intention, as these last two analyses show. A general principle seems to be that dreams very rarely deal with outside, important events in the world, but only with those that have a strong emotional value to the dreamer. Even wars only come up as expressions of man's aggressive tendencies.

The vast storehouse of the unconscious turns newly received information into a message of personal value. Just as we are serious one minute and silly the next, so our dreams reflect the gamut of human experiences. Take this example of a nationally significant event:

'I was invited to a reception at the home of Mr and Mrs Peter Phillips, parents-in-law of Princess Anne. When I got there, the place seemed very small: a thatched cottage of smaller-than-life size, with a large expanse of green grass in front. I went up to the door where Mr Phillips stood waiting to receive me. "Where's the marquee for the ball?" I asked. He laughed and said, "Oh, we're not having one, the party's out at the back." People seemed to be going through the house, but I turned into a room sort of tacked on to the side of the building. It turned out to be a very pretty, attractive child's bedroom with flowery wallpaper. A boy aged about twelve was asleep in bed. Somehow I knew it was Mark Phillips' younger brother, (although I know he hasn't really got one), but at the same time it was my own son. I was pleased about this, because it meant that I could check if he was all right, tuck him in and give him a cuddle.'

Scaling things down

This dream shows just how much more interesting than fact or fiction your dreams can be. The most obvious explanation is that the dreamer had been watching the wedding of Britain's Princess Anne on television the day before. This is reflected in the detail that some things seemed smaller than reality, like watching a little screen. The transformation into a cottage and the homelike detail 'It's out at the back'

brings the occasion down to a more immediate scale of values—a good example of the unconscious feeling that importance in social, public terms has little to do with genuine experiences of living. Incidentally, it echoes a happening in the dreamer's own life, for extensive building alterations were taking place at the back of her own house.

Motherly love

The final part of the dream is a picturesque and sincere expression of maternal care and affection. In the midst of this personally exciting occasion, the mother thinks of her child. It may seem unlikely, but puns in dreams are very common, and the whole association of royalty, and the 'marquee' bring to mind the picture of a little prince, (in French, *marquis*). It is a nice way of referring to one's offspring!

The bedroom

There may be more than sweetness and light in this apparently loving dream. Is there any significance in the situation of the bedroom just 'tacked on' to the house? It could be an expression of worry or doubt about the dreamer's way of combining her roles as a socially interested person and a dutiful mother. The dream gets round the problem by having a party and putting the child in the next room. Thus, any guilt feelings are overcome.

Looking for the answers

These dream samples demonstrate the enormous variety and depth of meaning that you can find in a superficially nonsensical experience. All the analyses show you how to progress, step by step, through the various stages of the dream. Clearly it is best to start your own efforts by contemplating complete dreams if you can.

Fragmentary recollections are more puzzling at first, but if all you have is 'snatches', then try to keep a record of them over days or weeks and then approach them with the same lines of thought shown here. The individual theories and meanings are described in depth in the sections following. You should always consider the pros and cons in your analysis. Do not write off a dream in one dimension, that is, 'Oh, this is pure wish-fulfilment/expression of fear/sexual fantasy/compensation/ etc . . .' Try to mull over all possible explanations. If you grow accustomed to this habit, then your final choice of an interpretation is more likely to be accurate, helpful and revealing.

Psychology and dreams: the theories

The pictures and stories presented to us in sleep are so strange and varied that it is not surprising to find so many different theories about their meaning. These range from the pure fantastical to the downright mechanical, comparing the mind to a machine.

The main reason for looking at the more important of these theories is that it helps to put your own ideas into perspective. Your interpretation will be more successful because you will have a solid background from which to work. You will be able to consider all the major factors that have been discovered about the world of dreams and to apply them to your own experiences.

Freud—the great innovator

One of the first great contributions to the study of dreams was made by Sigmund Freud. For many people he symbolizes the psychiatrist, the 'head-shrinker', more than any of the other famous names.

One possible explanation for this is the emphasis he laid on sex. All the cartoons showing patients lying on couches and doctors with notepads saying 'Tell me about your childhood' are based upon the Freudian view of psycho-analysis. He believed that everyone is born with basic urges which are suppressed as we grow up and learn to conform to society. So it can be helpful to go back and find out exactly when a certain urge was first curbed in childhood.

Perhaps some of Freud's ideas are laughable today—in stating his views, he had to exaggerate them; otherwise, no one would have paid any attention. If his theory about dreams seems 'sex-mad', consider that in a recent survey, 85% of the men admitted they had sexual dreams and 72% of the women agreed. It is the commonest of all dream subjects—and after all in real life, a good sexual relationship is one of the major reasons for a person's happiness and peace of mind.

What exactly did Freud believe? First, that all dreams are 'wish-fulfilling' of the sexual or aggressive impulses in human nature. These urges are with you from birth, but social training keeps them under control. Obviously,

to live in an ordered society you cannot go around gratifying your basic urges all the time.

Only in dreams, when your conscious mind is not on top of the situation, can these suppressed urges have a chance to come out. Freud believed this and explained why we dream in a different 'language'; not like real life, but doing absurd things with no clear sense of logic as we usually know it.

Because these urges are totally controlled by the conscious part of the mind, it is as if they can only be allowed out at night 'in disguise', using strange combinations of events and a secret sign language to get past the 'guard'— the conscious mind on patrol.

> 'There was a couple that I was watching. They were almost in silhouette. The girl was sitting semi-crossed legged, and the guy was sitting next to her and they were both naked. He just leaned round and touched her on the side of her hip, and she let out this incredibly sort of ecstatic sigh. Every time he touched her, she just went into an incredible convulsion and she started really arching her back. Then her legs came round and she just put her arm round him . . . it was very sensuous. Then she came round on top of him.'
> Motor mechanic, male, 22

The sexual sign language

Even if dreams do not appear to be about sex at all, Freud maintained that under the surface they invariably are. If a dream merely seems to pick out an event from yesterday or a recollection from the past, Freud thought that the incident was chosen out of all other possibilities because it linked up specifically with the urge being expressed in the dream.

Freud's list of sexual sign language seems endless: in the attempt to disguise the true nature of the dream, the unconscious uses a wide variety of

normal everyday objects to stand for sexual things: 'All elongated objects, such as sticks, tree trunks and umbrellas, may stand for the male organ, as well as long sharp weapons, such as knives, daggers and pikes. Boxes, cases, chests, cupboards and ovens represent the uterus and also hollow objects, ships and vessels of all kinds. Rooms in dreams are usually women.' With this means of disguise, the conscious is not alarmed and so allows us to sleep on peacefully. The 'watchful' part of the mind does not see through to the basic urge that is being expressed in a wish-fulfilling dream.

This theory may at first seem ridiculous but if someone has a sexual problem, it is more than likely that Freud's method will help to interpret their dream world. A young girl at college, worried about finding a boy-friend yet unsure of her ability to cope with sex, dreams of a large black gun firing off into a bare white room. There can hardly be the need for a psychoanalyst to help her see the wish-fulfilment suggested by that dream!

The sexual urge is very often expressed through other basic desires, like the appetite for food. Anyone watching the scene in the film *Tom Jones* in which the hero enjoys a frankly flirtatious meal with a loose lady must admit that their smacking of lips over the roast chicken hints at more than stomach hunger. In a dream, enjoying a meal with gusto can stand for an open, eager attitude towards satisfying sexual desires. A common type of man's dream goes like this:

> 'I walk into a beautiful dining chamber with glowing lights and a magnificent feast spread out on the table in the centre. Other people seem to be helping themselves freely to the food and wine, enjoying it all enormously. I want to go and help myself but cannot move forward. Finally a beautiful girl comes over and gives me a plate of food. I accept but, when I eat it, it tastes like liver and makes me feel sick.'

According to Freud, this dream represents a man's fear of sex—his inability

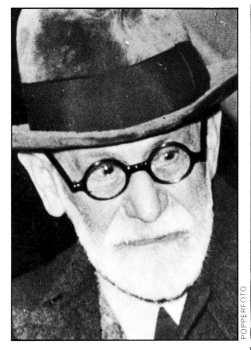

Sigmund Freud (1856-1939), born in Moravia, moved to Vienna at the age of four. His first passion was science, but he made medicine his career and explored the treatment of mental disorders. He dealt with people suffering from hysteria and soon developed the idea that by bringing to the surface the original reason or experience that caused a condition, the patient could be cured. This 'psychocatharsis' (*catharsis*: Greek for purging or cleansing) expanded into the field known as depth psychology or psychoanalysis.

He believed that the unconscious mind exerts a powerful influence over the conscious one and that fundamental instinctive urges are often coped with by pushing them out of sight or making them more socially acceptable by the process of 'sublimation'. More startling was his idea of 'infantile sexuality'; that is, from birth we experience sexual urges, at first directed solely towards the mother, who supports life.

His key work, *The Interpretation of Dreams* (1900), sets out his basic theories. Unlike Jung, Freud always maintained an 'analytical', scientific approach to the human personality, reducing problems to causes, which he saw sexually. This 'reductive' approach reduces the patient's present situation to its component parts through deep analysis of his past experiences.

Towards the end of his life, Freud gained wide recognition, especially in America. Because he was Jewish, Freud fled the Nazis in 1938. He settled in England and died the following year in London.

Alfred Adler (1870-1937) was born in Vienna, Austria, and after studying medicine became a disciple of Sigmund Freud. He defended Freud's views vigorously in the early days of their friendship but after nine years, his own ideas diverged from Freud's emphasis on the sexual urge underlying man's behaviour, and he set up an independent school of thought. Adler developed 'Individual Psychology', the study of people as goal-oriented individuals seeking personal perfection and wholeness.

His most significant theory was that everyone has difficulty in relating his own self-centred satisfaction and happiness to a contentment derived from fitting in to a group or society and his idea of 'will-to-power' led to wide acceptance of the 'superiority' and 'inferiority' complexes. Through dreams, Adler felt a person could better understand his aggressive impulses and desire for fulfilment. He sees what he really thinks of himself. The aim of Adlerian psychology is to help people fit their view of themselves into an acceptable social form. His studies were mainly concerned with the misfits of the world—criminals, drug-takers, drop-outs. He wanted to help people fit in. Freud and Jung were concerned with freeing the 'real' person inside and gave no emphasis to the world that this newly emerged self would find around him.

Adler achieved widespread recognition in his later years. He taught at Columbia University in New York City and at the Long Island College of Medicine, New York. He died on a lecture tour, in Scotland, in 1937.

Carl Gustav Jung (1875-1961) was a Swiss psychologist and psychiatrist. After studying in Basel and Paris, he became a disciple and friend of Sigmund Freud, the foremost psychologist of the time. After a few years, however, Jung developed a separate view and in 1914 formally broke away from Freud and his views. Jung took a much more religious, philosophical and mystical approach to the human personality than Freud's more scientific method, which delved into the root causes of problems.

Among Jung's contributions to the field of psychology was his explanation of the personality, or psyche, in terms of three systems that interact with each other. These are the conscious, the unconscious, and the 'collective unconscious'. The last was of great importance in explaining the meaning of dreams, for Jung was able to show that all people in the world show certain basic, inherited ideas, experiences or concepts expressed in eternal themes. These he called 'archetypes'. Jung was especially interested in mythology, alchemy, and world religions. During the 'thirties and 'forties he made various trips to Africa, Mexico, North America and the Far East to gather information and inspiration for his numerous books and essays.

Jung survived two world wars—he actually forecast the coming of the first in a vivid dream—and died in his homeland at Zurich in 1961.

JOHN GARRETT

Dreams can express repressed sexual fantasies and unconscious aggressive desires.

to find a happy sexual relationship. The fact that he sees everyone else around him enjoying it only makes him more inadequate and unable to cope. Interestingly the girl takes the first step, by giving him the plate of food (that is, making an advance). In real life, this man probably worries about girls a great deal, thinking they are a bit

> 'I am standing on a bank on the edge of water, but it isn't really water. I'm standing with my mother, my sister and my cousin. Then I dive in and as I dive in I look down my body and I've changed. I am now a girl with a female body in a black bikini. Then I hit the water and I come up and now I'm back to me again as a guy. I look up to the bank and everyone has blank faces and there are all sorts of breakers, breakers across the water. There are breakers all across the beach . . . like a beach I used to go to when I was a kid. I start walking down . . . but it carries on and gets a bit vaguer . . . it's no longer water, but in a building and I walk down into a room and then it becomes an old concert we had when we were at art college and I am in the cloakroom with Andy Fraser and people from the pop group Free. It's really weird. I recognize the room, but it's not the same and we are all standing there going, "Oh it's no good, it's not like it used to be".'
> Student, 20, male

'forward'. To tie in with Freud's view that personal recollection may support the sexual nature of a dream, it might turn out that the young man was often given liver as a child: his mother would say 'It's good for you, eat it up'. This would suggest a confused attitude about women, that he has not grown up sufficiently to be on his own feet and out of his mother's influence. (Freud believed that sexual feelings start with a child's desire for the mother in boys and the father in girls.) Perhaps the dream is also expressing the man's fear that if he does give way to his sexual urges, punishment will result as it did when he was a child.

Nowadays, people have a much broader view of sex and the Freudian view seems a bit one-sided at first. But in his lifetime during the late 19th century, young people (especially women) were brought up to regard sexual feelings or any other impulsive, natural outburst of emotion as socially forbidden. The upper middle classes of Vienna, where he lived and worked, were particularly straight-laced and admiring of controlled intellectual pursuits. No one spoke about feelings or passions and they were only given way to in deep secret, in the boudoirs and brothels inhabited by 'fallen' women. No wonder that most of Freud's patients were more confused and anxious about sexual feelings than anything else. His thoughts were naturally concentrated on this area and this is reflected in his findings.

A main difficulty with Freud's theory is that not all dreams are concerned with wish fulfilment. Later in his life, Freud too began to change his mind about this part of his work. Take the example given above: Freud's earlier interpretation would be more appropriate if the man in the dream took the plate of food from the girl, gobbled it all up, and asked her for more! The bad endings are explained by saying that the conscious mind on patrol is sufficiently alerted to these feelings coming out that it steps in and puts everything in order once again. It adds on the 'right' ending to crush the urge once more. In this way, Freud managed to keep up his theory that all dreams do express the wish-fulfilment of a basic sexual or aggressive desire.

The influence of Freud

Much of what Freud uncovered in his study of dreams has passed into our everyday life. A large proportion of film or television advertising is based on the wish-fulfilment principle. Just like a dream, the cigarette or alcohol promoter says, 'Here is an ideal world—fulfil your urge to be a sex king or goddess of love by using our product'. If you want some practice at recognizing objects with a Freudian sexual link, try studying the advertisements. Long sleek cars, full of power, that 'respond' to every command; 'satisfying' cigarettes, smoked by two in a field of corn; 'long cool drinks' in exotic places, followed by high dives into deep blue seas —the underlying sexual tone soon becomes very evident. What about those after-shave lotions that have women falling at the feet of judo champions? In these pictures, sex and aggression are very directly combined.

Letting off steam in dreams

Aggression is not necessarily the desire to go out and fight with guns or boxing gloves. In a much wider sense it means the basic drive for power or domination. Alfred Adler, one of Freud's best-known followers, expanded this view. He put forward the idea that everyone has an equally strong drive within them —the need to dominate. Furthermore, this usually springs from some basic inadequacy or lack which is subconsciously recognized at an early age. The rest of life is spent trying to compensate for it. Adler's theory has been popularized in such ideas as small men like Napoleon lusting for power or that bald men are very sexual to make up for their supposed lack of looks.

It may seem that both Freud and Adler take a fairly dim view of human nature. Their ideas are based on a sort of unending warfare between basic drives and the need to keep them under control. Letting these drives out in wish-fulfilling or power satisfying dreams is like letting the steam out of a kettle: if they are permanently bottled up, a severe nervous breakdown could result. So dreams provide a convenient escape valve.

This does not explain why many people actually wake up from their dreams. If the Freudian view was entirely right, then everyone would always sleep peacefully after a dream, having worked off some infantile wish or urge. But quite often the reverse occurs and we are very disturbed by the things that take place during dreams. It seems sometimes that a dream is acting as a voice of conscience, especially in terrifying dreams or nightmares.

Jung versus Freud

Carl Gustav Jung disagreed quite forcibly with Freud and his followers over this idea of dreams, as well as the view that repressed sexual or domination drives are the key to understanding the sign language of dreams. Jung saw clearly that Freud's great achievement was in drawing people's attention to the idea of the unconscious mind and how he related it to dreams. But he disagreed with Freud on a number of fundamental points. For one thing, Freud always used dreams as a way of getting back to the basic cause of a problem. Usually he found it in some important event in childhood—even in the moment of birth—which had affected the patient's view of himself throughout his life. Freud believed that unearthing the problem through psychoanalysis, including a discussion of a person's dreams, could often lead to a cure. Once the basic urge is recognized and coped with in real life, the obsession or fear produced by keeping it forcibly locked up inside would disappear.

For example, Freud describes a young man he once helped who had a morbid fear of going out in the street because he thought he would kill everyone in sight. It gradually emerged from his dreams and remembrances of childhood that he had at one stage heartily disliked his father, so much so that at the age of seven he had made a feeble but deeply-felt attempt to kill him. When his father eventually died the young man felt

very guilty, or rather felt that he should. He transferred his feeling to everyone outside and punished himself by locking himself up in his room all day. Once he recognized the urge dating back to early childhood, he was able to come to terms with his fear and greatly improved.

Jung however, took an entirely different view of dreams. He admitted that a great deal of what Freud had discovered was true, but he believed that the language of dreams was not just some secret code for basic drives, for wishes to be fulfilled. 'Going back' in Freud's way, seemed to reduce people's dreams to a set of rather unattractive, self-centred needs. He wondered why

Above: In dreams of a sexual nature it is interesting to see if natural or artificial images are used to express the dreamer's attitude.

dreams so often seemed to inspire people, to encourage them in their waking lives to do bigger and better things.

He was fascinated by the strange array of mysterious objects and creatures that occur in dreams. Freud's theory seemed to relate all parts of a dream to something inside the dreamer's own make-up. But to Jung this did not account for the pictures which appeared to come from a fantasy world outside the dreamer's everyday view of life.

28

Jung and the Collective Unconscious

Jung's solution to this mystery was that all human beings have two parts to their unconscious. Freud had looked at the part which hides personal, instinctive urges away. Jung now identified a part that is filled with strange primitive imaginings, which are common to everyone everywhere.

For example, why do all children love stories of witches, ogres and fairies when they have no real-life experience of these creatures at all? Why do people invent monsters in their dreams when there are no such things in the world? Jung suggested that we all share a Collective Unconscious, for we all respond to these basic fancies.

Many civilizations in all parts of the world have created exactly the same pictures in dreams, fairy stories and myths and they are readily understood by people from another country or from another age.

'I was sitting on top of Popocatepetl, playing a card game with three friends. Out of the volcano came beautiful soap bubbles which rose into the air, then floated down the conical sides of the volcano to join the sea of bubbles stretching away on every side as far as the eye could see. The sun came up and the bubbles glistened iridescently, first mauvy-blue, then peachy, then watery green, then all sorts of mother-of-pearl colours shimmering together.'
Student, female, 20

Throughout time, various nations have created remarkably similar stories about their heroes. Moses was found in the bulrushes; Jesus was born in an equally humble stable. The Greek goddess Aphrodite was born out of the sea just as the first ancient Inca ruler came out of a lake. There is no apparent reason for this similarity in legend, folklore and religion. Jung suggests that everyone has a natural tendency to think in these globally familiar ways.

Jung first drew attention to people's fascination with monsters. These fearful images seem to come from a universally shared mythology, equally recognizable to people from all civilizations.

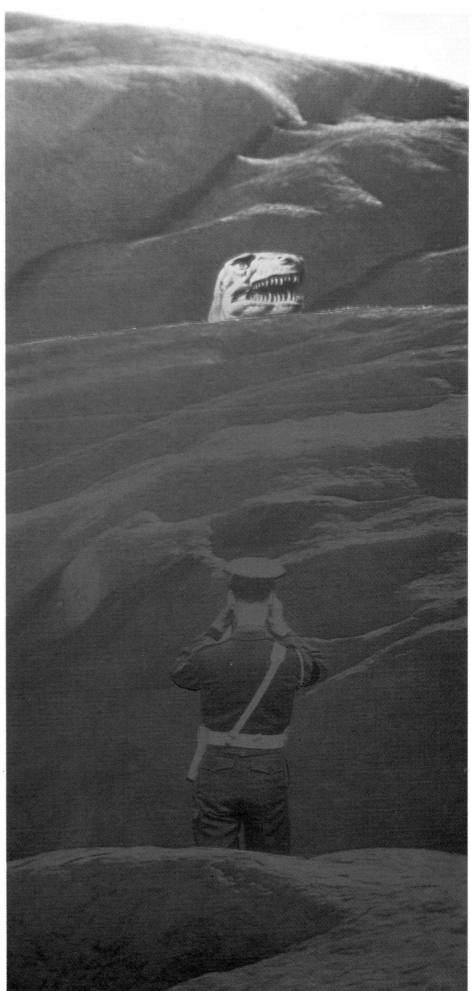

CHRIS YATES

Archetypes

These universal ideas were termed Archetypes, which means the original of a type. They are basic ancient beliefs which, according to Jung, we inherit rather than learn. So old and general are they that we do not need to ask what they mean when they appear in the mind's eye; we simply recognize them deep down without having to question them. These Archetypes are the language—the 'secret code'—of dreams.

Putting the theory into practice, look at the familiar figure of the hero. There are many instances in classical myths, such as the adventures of Hercules, Odysseus or Prometheus; in Britain there was the ideal of King Arthur and Sir Lancelot or St. George slaying the Dragon; in Australia Ned Kelly became a hero of mythic proportions, and there are countless examples from the Old West of the United States. Even in modern dress, the hero persists in comic strip characters such as Superman. Jung is simply saying that no one has to tell you what a hero is. You know what the person stands for as soon as you see the type.

Most of the Archetypes to which Jung drew attention were of a religious nature. Jung was for a long time Freud's disciple, and when he broke away from him because he disagreed with his views, he also developed a great interest in eastern religions. In turn people have disagreed violently with Jung, saying that this Collective Unconscious is a lot of mumbo-jumbo and cannot be proved scientifically. At least Freud had some factual basis for his beliefs. But in one sense the Jungian view is easy to accept, because he also believed that the Archetypes, as they appear in dreams, are reflections of ourselves. Many religions have a similar philosophy when they say God is really inside the individual.

But what if a dream contains a friend that you can recognize or even no people at all? Jung maintained that the friend is there because he or she reflects part of yourself. A room may stand for your own mind—the inside of yourself. In this way, all the Jungian Archetypes are simply representations of the human condition. Where they come from no one can say, but they are made concrete in the world of dreams, appearing like well-known actors on a private stage. Monsters are a 'projection', a representation of our own innermost fears. Heroes are a real-life realization of our own tendency to do good, brave deeds. A witchwoman—another familiar

Archetype—represents the destructive feminine impulse in human beings. Because these Archetypes are showing us to ourselves, they are easily recognizable, even by children. No one needs to explain to a child that the giant in Jack and the Beanstalk is all bad or that the Fairy Godmother in Cinderella is completely trustworthy. In the actual stories neither of these characteristics is proved: it is just known and accepted by the children hearing the tale. The same is true of the Archetypes of dreams. We do not read them up in books for they come naturally to mind. There is a mystery about the source of the Archetypes: if you are religious you will find it easy to believe that they spring from a force beyond human understanding. Others might accept that there is a basic energy in human nature which has over the

> 'My girlfriend and I are in a cottage in the country — not our real one, which stands by itself — but in one that is part of a group, but fairly isolated. There is a huge bomb explosion; the cottage of some people we know has been blown up and is burning ferociously. We know that they are dead, so we go indoors. But then we realize that the flames are spreading into our neighbors' houses, closer and closer to ours. I throw water on — and then buckets of pins and needles — to douse the flames. It is very powerful and scary.'
> Financial journalist, male, 32

centuries responded to certain unconscious forces. These are revealed in the Archetypes.

Archetypal symbols

One thing is sure—Archetypes occur time and time again in the same form. These are termed symbols. Just as a child instantly 'knows' the giant or the fairy godmother, so we all 'know' the meaning of the symbols. Take the story of the Garden of Eden. Eve is persuaded to eat an apple by an evil serpent. Everyone knows what the apple stands for, without having it spelled out for them. 'Forbidden fruit' is a symbol we can all understand. Another example is the standing stone. It is used to suggest permanence in many forms: in Stonehenge, in gravestones or in monu-

ments like the Cenotaph in London or the Washington Monument. In the Bible, Jesus calls his disciple Peter the 'Stone' or 'Rock', for that is the translation of his name from the Greek. Everyone recognizes the meaning behind the idea—even in today's conversation we refer to a reliable man with the phrase, 'He's as solid as a rock'.

Unknown Archetypes

More surprisingly, Jung discovered that people can dream using certain symbols without being at all clear of the Archetypal meaning at the time. People seem to inherit certain motifs in their thinking patterns without being aware of it. In one case, a girl dreamed of crossing a bleak moor with a good friend. On the way they met a large number of ape-like creatures with funny, friendly faces. They all proceeded together—arm in arm, cuddling up to the apes—towards their destination: a beautiful fairy-tale city glistening in the sunlight.

Only on thinking over the dream, which seemed to have no connection with any events in real life (no visits to the zoo!), did the girl discover that the ape-monkey is a very common symbol in eastern religions for the Self—the intuitive, emotional part of a person as opposed to the intellectual, logical part. A picture in a book of the Hindu monkey god Hanuman was so uncannily like the ape-monkey of her dream that the girl was very surprised. The friend was probably included in the dream because the dreamer admired her for her creative abilities and her warm personality. In Jungian terms, it all added up to a message that she should let the intuitive part of her nature guide her towards her goal—symbolized by the city—not just her thinking, logical self. Jung has written about many such incidents that occurred when he was treating his patients. If you cannot think of any private recollection connected with a symbol, it can be very helpful in your own attempts to understand dreams to try to find out something about the universal cultural symbolism described in the case above.

Anima or Animus: your dream reflection

Jung continued to explore the idea that dreams reflect the Self: one of the most fascinating ideas he put forward was that we have an opposite side to our personalities. In men, this appears as an idealized female figure called the Anima, in women, as a male, the Animus. In contrast, Freud would have believed that the appearance of a male

figure in a woman's dream represented sexual desires for someone, but Jung suggested that it could be the male aspect of her own character. We associate this with aggressive, extrovert, decisive qualities—some bad, some good. In a way, dreaming about male movie stars may even show a woman some aspect of her own male character. In men, the Anima is embodied in all the poets' ideas of an inspiring muse, who gives them the power to write beautiful things. In religion, she is the perfect figure of Mary, the mother of Jesus; in Chinese myth, she is the fertility goddess, Kuan-Yin; in classical times she was Aestarti, Venus or Ceres; nowadays she could be Marilyn Monroe, Maria Callas or even Queen Elizabeth II.

> 'I have a vast number of sales reports to make—but I haven't got round to it and I've forgotten what they're even supposed to be about. There's a great compulsion to get them done—but then suddenly I'm off on another business trip, involving a great deal of packing and preparation, none of which has been done and I have a ship to catch in a matter of hours. I always end up wondering whether I can conceivably get a car to get to the port on time.'
> Retired salesman, 60

The Persona and the Shadow

Two other parts of your self can appear in dreams in a symbolic form.
The first is the Persona, which Jung explains as the character or image you project outwardly. This acting figure who faces the world and says what it should do is often not your real self. In dreams, your Persona rather than your real self often takes part. You must recognize that this is not your innermost honest being. Jung tells the story of a woman who in real life was impossibly stubborn and full of fixed opinions. No one could ever win against her in an argument or even get her to admit she was wrong. One night she dreamed that she was going to a very important social occasion. On the doorstep, her hostess greeted her and said delightedly that all her friends were ready waiting inside. Then she led her through a doorway—into a cowshed! The dreamer's unconscious was giving her a picture of what her Persona

or image was really like and which she would not consciously admit to herself. Finally, a very helpful aid to understanding dreams from the Jungian point of view is contained in the Archetype of the Shadow. This is just what it suggests. It is the other side of your personality which does not see the light of day very often. It does not necessarily mean the evil or bad part of you, it might just be the secret part you feel least able to bring out into real life. It might be tender, imaginative and romantic and so you keep it lurking behind an agressive facade. It might also be truly destructive, as characterized vividly by Robert Louis Stevenson in *Dr. Jekyll and Mr. Hyde*—a story which came to the author during a dream.

The Shadow can be good or bad and can make your dreams very confused because you have to decide if the dream is about your outward personality or the Shadow behind. But life is pretty complicated too, and dreams reflect the conflicts experienced in it. It is interesting that small children seem to have an instinctive knowledge about the fundamental Archetypes of the Persona and the Shadow, for at some stage most play with an imaginary friend—who somehow seems to be the one who causes all the trouble in the household!

Although at first sight the theories of Freud and Jung seem to be poles apart and quite irreconcilable, they are not basically very contradictory. What matters most is that if a dream points out a problem area, exactly which way you take it will depend on your personal circumstances. Other symbols in the dream, especially those of a personal remembrance or of an Archetypal, general meaning, will help to make the central issue clear. Some people are more prone to follow Freud than Jung or the other way round. People who regularly visit a Freudian psychoanalyst tend to dream with lots of sexual pictures, while people who become interested in Jung start to fill their nights with magical visions of weird beasts and religious figures. The mind is very suggestive and responds to outside influences in surprisingly quick ways.

Dreams as problem solvers

Most modern dream researchers have established themselves on the basic principles of either Freud or Jung, and most have tried to find a less extreme position. J. A. Hadfield is a British psychologist who believes that dreams are basically problem-solving. He pays

particular attention to the fact that over a period of time, dreams will concentrate on a specific problem area trying out one possible solution after another until one dream comes to a realization of the issue. A simple example is the habit of dreaming about an accident. Drivers tend to have the same dream over and over again. At first the dream will make the accident take place as if realizing the dreamer's worst fears. Then gradually the content changes and the dreamer finally sees himself actually avoiding the accident by fast reaction and good steering. The dreams have worked off the driver's sense of anxiety and possible guilt about his behaviour on the road. So your dream may warn you where you are going wrong and why. It may reveal parts of yourself, consciously overlooked, which you should take into account in the future.

> 'I am on a paddle steamer— it's hot and sunny. Snow White and the Seven Dwarfs are sitting in deck chairs, surrounded by wicker travelling trunks. I go inside into a dim bathroom with no windows. The walls are covered with green tiles and the bulb is broken, leaving a glowing filament. Everything is dusty and dirty, and when I turn the taps on, rusty nuts and bolts come out.' Girl, 8.

Act out your dreams

An American psychoanalyst, Fritz Perls, developed the problem-solving aspect of dreams in an unusual way. One of his teaching methods was to have people act out the events of their dreams as if they really happened. It can be surprisingly revealing, and sometimes very amusing to do this.

Perls once had a teenage girl patient who had dreamed several times about her mother but had no idea what the drift of her thoughts intended. She thought she had a good relationship with her mother, all things considered. Perls asked her to talk as if she were the mother-figure in the dream and then to reply as the daughter. It rapidly emerged in this invented conversation that the voice she gave the mother was louder, more decisive and altogether more on top of the situation. As 'herself', the girl seemed unable to reply and changed physically as she acted, hanging her head and mumbling her words. Clearly, the girl did not really feel that she had found her feet. Nor was she free of her mother's domination, although she had said aloud that she got along with her mother pretty well. She automatically assumed the hangdog, feeble Persona of her dream.

You can try this simple experiment yourself—even if the dream is about objects, not people. For instance if the dream has a tree in it, why not imagine what kind of tree *you* are: 'I'm a tall thin sapling. I may not look very strong, but actually I can withstand winds and rain well, because I can bend and not break'. Over a period of time, you can build up a very revealing commentary, especially if you keep a journal of these thoughts.

The off-line brain

If however you dislike the idea of so much imagination being involved in understanding your dreams, you may prefer to consider the very interesting theory put forward by another British specialist, Dr. Christopher Evans. Remember that the unconscious has been described as a 'sorting house', taking in all kinds of information, sifting and absorbing it and then telling you in a dream how things stand in your real self. Dr. Evans has developed the idea of the sorting-house into a comparison with a computer. A computer is just a very elaborate calculating machine whose operation is controlled by large numbers of 'programs'. Programs are nothing more than special instructions which tell the computer what to do. With modern computers these programs have to be continually revised and brought up-to-date, a process which is best done when the system is (to use a technical term) 'off-line'. When a computer is off-line it is not switched off but rather uncoupled from its environment. Plenty of activity can go on inside but it doesn't interact with the external world. You might say that it's a little like a library which is put out of bounds to the public at regular periods so that the staff can do some cataloguing and rearranging. If computers don't have their programs revised in these off-line periods then they get muddled, out-of-date, inefficient and ultimately breakdown. Dr. Evans argues that the brain itself is a computer—a biological rather than an electromechanical one—and it too must be controlled by programs. Furthermore these programs must also be revised and updated and this must be done when the system is 'off-line'. So when we are asleep our brain is off-line and dreams represent the brain sifting through its

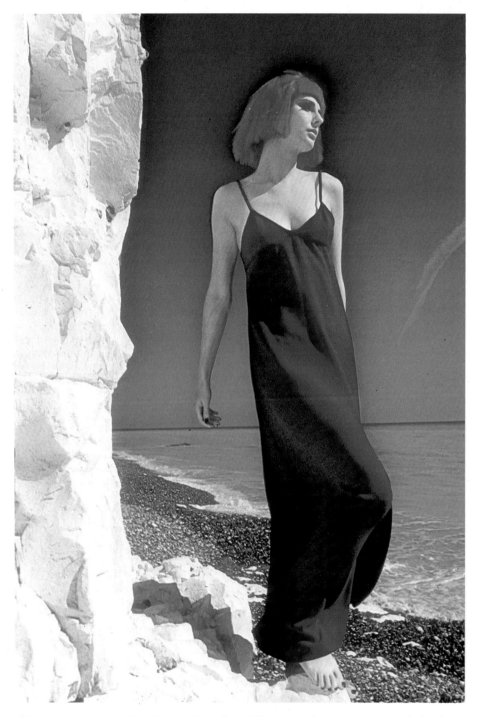

old programs, rewriting them, discarding dud ones and putting in new ones. We do this, Dr. Evans believes, for a large part of the sleeping period and it is this program revision that is the basis of true dreaming. The kind of 'dreams' we remember over breakfast in the morning are the fragments of the major programs which were being rewritten during the night and which were interrupted for one reason or another as the conscious mind briefly came awake.

If you look at each individual incident or object in a dream, it will relate to some new information, some newly-absorbed experience in your recent past. It might be from words read in a newspaper, from pictures seen on

Women in dreams may not only be the subject of sexual fantasy, but alternatively a symbol of the feminine aspects of a man's nature.

television, overheard remarks or friendly conversations. All these bits and pieces will be sifted and processed by the computer-brain in sleep.

All these theories, old and new, are evidence of the vast amount of research that is going on at present to understand the significance of dreams. No matter which view appeals to you most, at least consider that dreams are not completely random and absurd. They are proof that the brain is a complex, delicate organ with a potential that has barely been recognized.

The language of dreams

Dreams give their message in a direct, non-verbal way: they present a series of ideas inside your sleeping brain. Some of the ideas come in a very clear visual sequence which you can recall in the morning and relate to someone else almost as if the whole experience had really happened or had been read as part of a book. At other times the pictures are so fragmentary and jumbled that you can only remember one particular action.

Psychologists attach a great deal of importance to the way things are presented in dreams. To understand the message, it is vital to know what to look for. For instance, if someone you are talking to yawns while saying 'how interesting' and looks over your left shoulder, he is trying to tell you that the whole subject is really a bore. Dreams often use the same mannerisms we use in conversation and these tricks of speech give a clue to what is really being conveyed.

The meaning of symbols

First, learn to distinguish between symbols and images in your dreams. They are both dream pictures, but the possible meanings are very different. Symbols say something to everyone. They have a general significance which can be grasped by all people everywhere.
The 'magic man' is a traditional symbol, of which many examples can be found. Merlin the Magician, the Wizard of Oz, the witch-doctors of Africa or the medicine men of American Indian tribes have the same powers.
The Garden of Paradise is another well-known symbol. This is a vision of a perfect place where everything is good and nothing goes wrong. People of all eras have found ways to express this symbolically. There is the Garden of Eden in the Bible, the Elysian Fields of Greek myth, and Mahomet's beautiful Paradise of the Islamic faith, where lovely girls or 'houris' wait with musk perfume, wine and the promise of love for the faithful. Nowadays, the same ideal is used by travel brochures to lure holidaymakers to that perfect resort where the sun always shines, the sea is clear and blue, the beach isn't crowded

and there's a never-ending supply of exotic food, drink and beautiful people.
A ship sailing over an empty ocean symbolizes man's progress through life. It is a good example of combining more than one symbol to form a widely-understood situation. The ship represents his society—his way of organizing with other people, some system against possible chaos in the world. The sea stands for the age-old unknown forces of the universe or the creative mass which lies unformed below the surface of the mind. This way of imagining life

> 'I set out on a journey with a large open egg tray balanced on the palm of my hand and a carafe of wine clutched in the other. The terrain was rocky and the narrow footpath lined with bushes. The pace was brisk and I had to concentrate very hard not to break the eggs as I tripped up and down the uneven path. When I got to my destination the eggs just broke of their own accord. I thought: "Well I still have the wine". Then I noticed I no longer had it. Concentrating so hard on the eggs, I had left the wine somewhere along the way. So I turned back to find it.'
> **Fashion journalist, 36, female**

comes to us in the stories of Odysseus travelling the seas in search of home or in Jason's hunt for the Golden Fleece. In the Middle Ages, the 'Ship of Fools' was a favourite theme, characterizing all the types of people you could meet on your journey through life. Perhaps the familiarity of this symbol accounts for its favour with politicians, who are constantly talking about the 'ship of state' and the need for a 'firm hand at the helm'.
If you find something in your dreams that is not clear to you from your own experience of life or from immediate past events you can recall, then try to think more broadly of its possible symbolic meaning. The paradise sym-

bol just mentioned is quite common. Any dream of a beautiful calm place, not necessarily a Garden of Eden in the religious sense, may have overtones of this general symbolic meaning. Sailing on a ship may have nothing to do with sea voyage you have actually experienced: it may simply be a way of representing your progress through life. The phrase 'all at sea' will perhaps help you to understand the function of this symbol.

Images in dreams

An image works rather differently from a symbol. This is simply a more accurate way of referring to a picture. Dreams work in images: they take an idea, a thought or feeling and turn it into an exact picture or image to present to you in sleep. They are generally more commonplace than symbols—like offices, shops and all the paraphenalia of day-to-day life. This word is properly used in the phrase, 'He's the spitting image of his father'—that is, he looks exactly like him.
Suppose someone is 'up in the clouds' in your opinion. In your dream, you may well have an image of him actually sitting on a cloud. Studying hard for exams might show up in a dream as someone being force-fed or sitting in front of a huge plate of food. When you 'can't take any more in', your dream says so with an image of the feeling. If you feel you cannot see the wood for the trees in your life, perhaps you will dream of being lost in a giant forest.
Not all dreams are just images of well-known phrases like this: sometimes your dream invents a new image or picture as a way of saying something. Men who have trouble relating to women often dream of she-monsters. This is a vivid image of their feelings, showing how they respond emotionally to the female. Their shyness may really be a fear that women are too clever or too passionate and will take them over completely.
Images can be very amusing because they are so apt and direct in their message. A young girl who was beginning to visit a psychoanalyst to work out a particular difficulty in her life

Above: Background in dreams is very
important. Exotic, faraway places
suggest freedom and a lack of inhibition.
A desirable and inviting girl is of
course a standard male fantasy!

dreamed that she arrived at her analyst's house and found lots of underwear
all over the waiting room. It was being
aired on the radiators and on chairs
round the heater. This could be interpreted as an image of the girl's own
misgivings about 'washing her dirty
linen' in public, expressing a wish that
her analyst would spill a few secrets in
return just to even the balance! Of
course, this is just one possible interpretation: remember that the image of

ladies' underwear has strong sexual
overtones as well.

The tricks of dream language

Once you can begin to look at the
apparent 'story' of your dream as a
series of images, then you will find it
much easier to study. Try to evaluate
each picture in its own right, as well as
the overall effect of the dream. When
you recognize images and see the
possible symbolic value of some of them,
then you can try to supply the following
advice about the tricks or mannerisms
of dream language. These points to
watch were first recognized by Sigmund
Freud, whose book, The Interpretation

of Dreams is still considered to be one of
the finest and most valuable studies in
the field.

Condensation

More than likely, you have already
discovered that any one image in a
dream can mean a number of things.
Do not worry or be put off if several
different ideas spring to mind at once it
only shows how rich in suggestion and
how powerful in meaning the dream
language can be. Freud had one fascinating example of this characteristic,
which he called condensation. A woman
dreamed about some beetles trapped in
a small box. At first she thought the

35

image had been suggested by something she had seen the day before—a moth had fallen into a glass of water. This might indeed have provoked the choice of image but does not go deep enough into why, of all the petty details from the day, that should have come up in her dream. The woman was then reminded of her daughter's hobby of collecting butterflies and this drew her back to memories of her own youth. Finally, Freud helped her to work through to the hidden or latent meaning of her dream. She was concerned about her husband's waning interest in sex and she knew that a well-known aphrodisiac called *cantharides* is made from crushed beetles.

Another image in the dream helped the woman to put two and two together, for she had also dreamed about open and shut windows. This immediately reminded her of a running battle she had with her husband about fresh air in the bedroom, rather than all the windows being shut. That led to a consideration of her relationship with her husband, and the underlying meaning of the beetle image came clear.

What if you do not know all the possible meanings of an image? After all, not everyone knows about aphrodisiacs made from beetle juice! The woman worked round to her own meaning simply by seeing connections—or condensations—in the beetle image of her dream. Thinking about her daughter's hobby reminded her of her own youth and attractiveness and called back memories of old romances. This in itself would have led to the heart of the problem, even if she had stopped there with the beetle image. Remember also that dreams are more often than not about things that worry us. It is not usually necessary to dig very deeply before the problem springs to mind. It is only in serious cases of mental anxiety or disturbance, when the cause is buried in the unconscious, that a lot of pain and effort is required to find it— and that calls for professional help.

Displacement

Almost as important as the condensing process is displacement, when the real concern of the dream is pushed into a small image. The images are skirting round the issue in order to avoid presenting a direct, head-on picture of the problem. If the dream becomes too clear it often turns into a nightmare

Left: The mood generated in a dream is very significant. The landscape could be gentle but is there an air of menace?

which wakes the dreamer up. Freud also thought that dreams are thus disguised to avoid upsetting the 'Conscience' part of the mind—the part that guards the basic thoughts and tries to stop them coming out—but nowadays, like most of Freud's ideas, this view is disputed.

Suppose you are worried about a relative, such as your sister. You might dream of a woman being involved in a car crash. This stranger may look totally different from your real-life sister, except that she is wearing the same glasses or a dress in a style your real sister prefers. This should be enough to tell you the true subject of your dream.

Freud was right in saying that this displacing device occurs when a part of you thinks you are doing something wrong. Suppose you are attracted to someone but you think should not be. You may have a very sexy dream involving a complete stranger, but his name may be similar, his clothing—or even a word he says—may recall the true object of your feelings. But if this were always true, then you would never have very explicit, clear dreams whose questionable parts are not disguised, and you would wake up far less often than you do from disturbing dreams.

A stranger or a shadow in a dream, incidentally, may have some symbolic meaning as discussed in the previous chapter. These figures can stand for sides of your own nature or personality that you do not know or refuse to acknowledge. Obviously, the other images in a dream will help you to decide which is the correct way of assessing them.

Reversal

An amusing trick to try, if a dream obstinately refuses to yield any meaning to you whatsoever, is to turn it round completely. Reversal is a common feature of the dream language. If you dream you are walking over a carpet in muddy boots, then why not consider: 'Am I the carpet, being walked over by other people?' The dream image may be saying, 'Don't be a doormat', in an upside-down way. The feeling of the dream may help. You would probably feel upset or indignant during a dream of this sort, which would certainly reflect the true meaning.

Killing or harming a child in a dream is a common worry for parents. But this too might be reversal; they hope very much that no harm of any sort will come to the family. But according to Freud, it might also be a wish-fulfilling

dream, recalling some moment of intense exasperation when a parent does feel like 'killing' a child. It is better to let off steam in this way in a dream than to harbour the feeling so that it affects your real experience of life.

Killing your own father or mother however does not follow the reversal principle. This merely shows in strong terms your attempts to break away from parental authority. You want to stand on your own feet and be independent. A parent can be concealed in an image of another kind of authority—a king, a ruler of a state or your boss at work.

A more Jungian approach might also consider whether you wish to rebel against some dominant part of yourself, reflected in an authoritative person.

Compensation

Jung also elaborated on the idea of reversal, believing that one of the main functions of a dream is to provide compensation for your real self. If you are a harrassed housewife, you may dream of being a glamorous, cool career woman. A ruthless businessman will tend to put himself in the place of a butterfly collector or a romantic intellectual in an ivory tower. A shy girl will dream of holding court in a circle of admiring boys. All these dreams are making up for the failings or unfulfilled needs of an everyday self.

Animism

Bear in mind also that if a person in your dream seems particularly wonderful, magical or idealized, it may come under one of those symbolic meanings already discussed.

A very beautiful, tender woman in a man's dream might represent his own finer, female instincts—what Jungian's call the Anima. Similarly, a sympathetic, courageous male figure might stand for a woman's own braver nature —her Animus.

Dreams have a habit of showing abstract things or feelings in the more visual form of people or animals. Bravery, just mentioned, will become a brave man; tenderness, a loving woman; Freud called this trick 'animism'. The same term is often used to describe the way objects are given human or animal properties by primitive peoples, for in their waking, day-to-day life they too turn abstract things into people or animals. The wind becomes 'the big man who blows'. Try to think broadly about this kind of image in dreams, for they work in the same way.

A **policeman** is often the most familiar character to appear in our dreams as the voice of conscience.

A **devil figure** may represent feelings or urges which you think are wrong but somehow cannot control.

An **angel** will act as the voice of good, as if from the nobler side of your nature or from your heartfelt faith in something.

A **tramp** will be an image for some unacceptable part of you or for something of which you are ashamed.

A **gipsy** will stand for some wild, impulsive, out-of-the-ordinary desire that you have lurking about inside you.

A **baby** will not just stand for birth or for your own desire to have children. It can just as well signify abstract things such as ideas or creative imaginings. A good example of this was a young man's dream about giving birth to perfectly-formed but very small babies. It was not some peculiar urge to be a woman! His profession was graphic designing and the babies stood for his wish to produce 'perfectly conceived' finished artwork or design ideas.

The cat image normally stands for supposedly feminine qualities such as intuition.

Dogs not unnaturally act as images for more traditionally masculine attributes such as adventurousness, aggression or faithfulness. This is an image that can contain many different abstract references, so you have to consider your own particular view of dogs (especially pets you know well) and add those ideas to the suggestions given here. For example, a scruffy, mongrel-type dog could indicate a low opinion of someone—possibly yourself—coming out in your dreams.

Other animals that commonly occur as dream images are wolves (fear, sexual aggression, hunger), rats (despicable, underhand people or feelings), rabbits (fertility or soft, easily-hurt characters) lambs (sacrifice, innocence, purity) and sheep (easily swayed, timid people). Sometimes the very nature of an animalistic image will help you to see the true meaning.

Horses for example are frequently chosen by female dreamers to symbolize the act of sex. A wild, strong stallion with a flowing mane is a beautiful way of imagining the power and force of sexual feeling. Notice how different this is from that other favourite sexual symbol—the automobile.

The car is sleek, powerful and shiny, but it is also automatic and mechanical underneath. If you dream of being driven by someone or sitting in the passenger seat, this indicates a more

passive role in the situation. You should look into the dream to see if taking a more positive, outgoing attitude is being suggested to you.

Jokes and puns

Not all dreams take a serious approach to your experiences. For some reason, people find it difficult to accept jokes or puns in dreams at first, as if they believe that dreams must always be intense, mysterious and earnest underneath. But some unusual experiments have proved that we use word-play even in sleep.

> 'I was wearing a backless bathing suit and I had to have a school photograph taken in those strange rows they make you sit in. For some reason I had a bra on underneath — and as the costume was backless you could see the bra at the back. So I wanted to find a place to take it off, just a public lavatory or something. But either I couldn't find one or if I got to one, there was always someone waiting outside and I was feeling a bit coy about the whole thing, so I was having a terrible time. I think I eventually did get the bra off and I felt much happier, then I went and sat down in my place with an enormous sweater over the bathing suit so that the whole thing was pointless anyway, with sort of little pink knees showing and wondering whether anyone would mind about the fact that I didn't have a school dress on.'
> Package designer, female, 24

Ian Oswald, the British dream researcher, describes how the whispering of certain names to sleeping people, for instance the name of an ex-girlfriend or a former work colleague, will draw a response from the dreamer. A girl who heard the word Robert inserted a rabbit into her dream! The brain seems to mishear the word and includes an image whose word sound is close to the word actually said. Don't dismiss word-play or punning when looking for the meaning of a dream image. Someone who places the events of a dream in a football field for instance may in fact mean 'field' in its metaphorical sense,

as in the 'field' of medicine or academics.

Psychologists find that people sometimes see a joke that is not apparent to anyone else. The dreamer recognizes that a figure represents someone known personally, because of a silly word or a ludicrous situation. If a dream contained the image of a king seated on a throne in the act of re-folding the Sunday newspaper and grumbling about it, then a family member might know instantly that the royal figure was Dad, who always complained about everyone else getting the paper first and losing his sports page!

Absurd dreams

An extension of dreams with jokes or puns are those which are at the time absurd. You wake up thinking, 'What a silly situation!' Sometimes the absurdity is simply the result of a lack of time-span or proper connections. This is a characteristic of dreams in general. They are like films that are badly made, jumping suddenly from one scene to the next, from one image to another without proper observance of the conventional logic of real life. This explains why dreams often contain absurd mixtures of people. Suppose your grandfather is mixed up in a dream with some of your close friends and neighbours, when in reality he died ten years ago. Freud suggests that this is as if you were saying to yourself, 'What would my grandfather say about this if he were alive?' Your dream, with no respect for time or individuals, simply makes that suggestion real. Even if you can't imagine why you should think such a thing—even unconsciously—stop and wonder if there are any characteristics about your grandfather (or whoever it is) that have some relation to the subject matter of your dream. It can be quite revealing.

Although it is sometimes upsetting or distressing to dream about a relative or dear friend who is dead, this explanation will help to put it into perspective. You may be bringing that person back because they held views or values that

Nudity is an expression of a desire to be frank and open without hiding behind a social facade. It can turn up in the oddest situations—but are they really so absurd? A tiger for instance is a clear image of the power of sexuality; a policeman and obviously a priest stand for the force of conscience. In this context, death, in the form of a funeral cortège, could stand for the dreamer's suppression of real feelings.

are significant in your present life. However, Freud also points out that ridicule can be a form of criticism. If you place someone near to you in an absurd position then you may be letting out some critical opinion you formerly kept to yourself, possibly for the best of reasons, like love or a sense of respect. Do not confuse absurd dreams with others which are simply odd or peculiar. Absurd dreams have a strong feeling of mockery attached to them *at the time*. You often feel that things are absurd during the dream itself. Most dreams only seem silly when you wake up and think about them in the cold light of day.

Nakedness. A common dream of this type that causes embarrassed laughs is that of nakedness. 'I walked right down the main street in broad daylight with nothing on, but I didn't seem to care.'

The interesting point to notice is the lack of any sense of absurdity or shame at the time. Freud believed these dreams were purely wish-fulfilling, satisfying a basic exhibitionist streak in everyone. However, Jung and many other psychologists have come to accept this kind of image as an expression of a desire to be frank, open and true to ourselves. If there is any feeling of fear attached to it, then clearly the message is that you are afraid of what people might think if you express your real views, behave naturally or lower your defences.

It is interesting to see how social convention makes us think that being stripped or caught without clothes is a sign of humiliation, shame or degradation. This dream image is really using the idea in a much more basic, true way. How about the traditional story of

'Lion devouring a horse' by the celebrated 18th century British painter, George Stubbs, is a powerful impression of the destructive capacity of aggressive or sexual drives. Both animals are world-wide symbols of these instincts.

the Emperor's new clothes—is it a joke against the court who fell for appearances, or against the Emperor for being so silly that he walked about in the nude?

Swimming is frequently connected with nakedness dreams. By now you will probably be thinking ahead to its possible meanings. People talk about being 'in the swim', or in old-fashioned schoolgirl slang, things went 'swimmingly'. Add to this the ideas already explained about the sea or ocean symbol and it is easy to see that swimming represents being at ease with life or being at one with your feelings and desires, pushing ahead with energy and excitement. Adler would say that swimming with effort stands for the urge for power or achievement; thus swimming upstream or against the tide can be taken exactly as the words suggest. You are going against popular opinion or trying to cope with troublesome issues. If the dream includes reaching land after the struggle, it may be a way of encouraging you in your aims.

Naked swimming can also suggest sexual fulfilment, as you will no doubt know if you have ever watched those old films with native girls splashing around, wide-eyed and flower-decked, while gun-laden soldiers or pith-helmeted hunters peer through the bushes! (Freud also said a great deal about the sexual imagery of guns and other weapons.)

Repetition

At the opposite end of the scale from absurdity or apparent nonsense is the intense feeling that is generated by repetition. This way of making a point in a dream is the most easy to identify. It is explained simply as a way of saying 'very much so' in images.

Climbing up a hill which seems endlessly steep and arduous is a way of saying 'Getting along in this life is very, very hard going'. It could be that the dream is an expression of fear or doubt about a particular goal you have in sight. You might pause and consider if pursuing the aim is really as important as all the effort it will cost.

A very long journey by train or bus embodies the same idea. 'Life is tedious', the dream is saying. It is implicit in the train image that catching or missing it relates to your views about life. Are you missing out on good opportunities; do you worry about success? An endlessly repeated attempt to catch a train would suggest a state of anxiety or tension about getting on in the world. Perhaps the dream is warning you to relax a little and not take things so seriously. Remember that mechanical means of transport also suggest an automatic, driving power in your life. We say someone has 'gone off the rails' if things go wrong for him. An endless train journey, especially if you are a passive individual sitting quietly in a carriage watching everything flit by, suggests a humdrum existence in which you let yourself be carried along. But your dream is telling you that somewhere deep down you know this is not really what you want.

Lucid dreams

Sometimes you will have a dream in which you are passive in a different way. You stand back from the events taking place, saying to yourself, 'I *know* this is a dream, but I'll let it go on'. Other people decide exactly the same thing but enter the dream, changing what happens in it. It is as if they say, 'I don't like this part of the dream; let's change it to something else'. These are called lucid dreams and offer two possible explanations. If you realize it is a dream but stand back and do nothing, then this is a way of keeping the situation at arm's length. You do not enter into the experience of the

> 'I remember sitting in a cafe with a friend. The cafe is a very strange place with lots of different levels and stairs. The table we are at is beside a window which looks out over a large walled garden. The garden seems quite a long way down and is ablaze with flowers and plants of every description. Suddenly I am no longer in the cafe but in the garden, there are lots of loaves of bread about. Then I see a large, green crocodile. I start to climb the wall, which is easy (but I seem to be getting nowhere fast). I eventually reach the top and find myself in a wasteland. I wander off and walk miles until I come to a river. There is a bridge over the river and I see a policeman and another man.'
> **Illustrator, 25, female**

problem even in sleep. This might be a way of showing that in reality you behave in just the same way—by not facing up to issues or meeting them head-on.

If on the other hand you seem to direct the course of the dream, changing the 'plot' and making things happen, then it is possible that the dream is being helpful or therapeutic. You are exploring various endings or trying out different ways of resolving your real-life difficulties. Dreaming of making things come to life exemplifies the kind of image found in a lucid dream. It is a beautiful way of suggesting that there are latent, unused powers inside you that are beginning to blossom and come out. You should be encouraged by such

a promising dream and act on it as positively as you can!

Secondary revision

The final point to consider when you are looking at dream images is a little more complicated but worth the effort if you find that most dreams respond to your analysis, but just a few evade you. It often happens that a dream seems so clear and recognizable that the meaning is straightforward and comes out at once. This is especially likely if the dream has similarities with a wish or favourite ambition. Knowledge of these ideal hopes and fantasies keeps a public relations man's salary healthy, when he plays up to them in his advertisements! Suppose you dream of moving into a beautiful house, furnished in exquisite taste with everything you have ever wanted. Whatever else happens in this dream, you will be likely to wake up and say, 'Oh well, that's clear, it was just one of my wish-fulfilling dreams', and then forget all about it. Of course you want a house like that—many people do. But dreams are rarely quite so simple. You will probably overlook other parts of the dream in order to fit the whole experience into your favourite fantasy. Freud described this process as 'secondary revision' and maintained that it leads people into making quick, superficial judgements about the contents of their dreams. Look more closely at that house again. Were there any details, such as going down into the basement or climbing upstairs to look at the view? Were there any objects you noticed as you passed—any clothes in cupboards or rubbish left neatly in a corner?

It may not always work, because dreams fade so quickly, especially if you made a quick snap judgement and put the thought aside. But if you can go back over the dream and look at the finer details, you will probably surprise yourself as new interpretations spring to mind.

Looking into your dreams

Do not worry if you feel you will not remember all these different points when you try looking at your own dreams. Even if you only remember one or two the first time, the rest will follow. It is much better to take a relaxed view and simply mull over a few thoughts. You will certainly fail if you sit down with a long list and a red pencil, taking an academic approach to the task. Dreams are natural things and they should not be forced into an intellectual guessing game.

What is sleep and how do we dream?

When you go to sleep you do not merely lose awareness of the world around you. Pronounced physiological changes also take place. The body's temperature is lowered, the heart's pulse rate is slower, and various bodily functions such as digestion are measurably reduced.

It seems that there could be certain areas of the brain which need constant stimulation to keep us awake that is, conscious. Sleep is the state which occurs when these areas cease to be stimulated.

No one can survive without regular periods of sleep, even though it may seem a waste of time—especially to children—to spend about a third of a lifetime in what appears to be a state of 'nothingness'. Furthermore, sleep is required *at regular intervals*: it is not as useful to the body to have 4 hours of sleep one night and 30 hours the next. The body has learned to work by a 24-hour clock and finds it difficult to forget. This clock, based on the movement of the earth round the sun and the consequent periods of light and dark, is known as the 'circadian rhythm'.

There is some truth in the general belief that working on night shift produces less satisfactory work than the normal daytime periods. The body takes many days, even weeks, to get out of the circadian rhythm, and during that time physical co-ordination, alertness and other manifestations of mental ability function less effectively. Anyone who has travelled between continents by jet will know how difficult it is to adjust to a new time scale. Even the relatively simple 'hop' between New York and London means a 5-hour difference in time and many people feel disoriented for several days, even if they appear to have caught up with lost sleep.

In general, the brain needs regular doses of sleep to continue making judgements or decisions and carry on other thinking processes. Experiments have shown that sleeplessness does not impair physical activity—but it does hinder concentration. People become increasingly vague the longer they go without sleep, eventually suffering from hallucinations—literally dreaming with their eyes open.

The activity of sleep

When asleep, the body and brain are not completely dead to the world or unconscious. The body is kept going by the activity of the autonomic nervous system, which controls the essential 'life support systems' of the heart, digestion, cell repair and replacement and so on, which continue during sleep. The senses also continue to be active to a certain degree: when an alarm clock rings, a part of your head registers the sounds of the bell and responds to the stimulus, sometimes dragging you unwillingly from sleep. A mother can be woken by her small baby crying to be fed at 2 am, while other people in the house—even the baby's own father—will not be disturbed.

Another part of the brain allows us to ignore regular noises, like cars outside or mild rainstorms. In this way even while asleep the brain apparently selects the intake of stimuli and lets us respond to some, but not to all. You can actually exploit or train your mind to some degree: many people say to themselves, 'I must get up early tomorrow' and actually wake up even before the alarm clock rings. Routine can play its part, for you can accustom yourself to waking regularly at 7 or 8 am if this is part of a long standing pattern of living. In the same way, many people always feel hungry at noon or at six.

Orthodox sleep

The activity of the brain during sleep is of course very important when studying dreams. Scientists have found that it is possible to measure brain activity by measuring the electrical impulses constantly given off. These can be registered on a machine called an electro-encephalograph (*cephalos* being the Greek work for 'head'), known as an EEG machine. By attaching electrodes to people's heads in various special spots, an interesting record of brain activity can be obtained. It seems that adults have several levels of sleep. At first, while someone is fully awake but preparing for sleep, a steady wave pattern is detected by the EEG machine. These waves are called 'alpha rhythm'. This is not exactly the same as being wide-awake and fully alert, for if the telephone rings or some other circumstance forces a person to get out of bed, these alpha waves disappear, and a completely different pattern is recorded.

After this first 'alpha rhythm' stage, the brain falls into a second stage of drowsiness, and a pattern of much slower, more irregular waves occurs. Then, finally, the person falls into deep sleep, characterized on the EEG machine by big, deep 'delta' waves, punctuated by small patches of shorter, faster waves, which are termed 'sleep spindles'. This state is known as 'orthodox sleep'.

During sleep, people fluctuate from one level to another, rising up and down through the three main stages in 90-minute cycles. So on average (although this is very rough and does not allow for the immense variety in sleeping habits that has been found), most people have three or four periods of deep, big-wave sleep each night.

Although people tend to think that deeper sleep comes late in the night, there is some evidence to show that the brain derives the most refreshment and benefit from the big-wave levels of sleep that occur in the earlier cycles of the sleep period. It also seems that the first hour or two of sleep goes immediately into the 'delta' wave level. So

Right, above: 'Stop-frame' photography has shown that the body changes position constantly during sleep. Below: The EEG machine records the electric impulses generated by the brain during sleep. Electrodes are also attached to pick up the muscular movement of eyes, throat and heart.

The first 10 minutes of sleep		NREM sleep	REM sleep
Awake – (Alpha waves)	Stage 2	eyes quiescent	rapid eye movements
Stage 1	Stage 3 (NREM sleep)	EEG: big, slow waves	EEG: low voltage waves
		throat muscles tense	throat muscles relaxed
		heart regular	heart irregular

perhaps there is some truth in the saying that sleep before midnight is better than sleep in the early hours—if a person's usual time for going to bed is about 10 pm. But obviously if someone is accustomed to sleeping from midnight until 10 am, he will draw the greatest benefit from his sleep between midnight and 2 am. In the same way, you do not necessarily need double sleep to recuperate from a very late night. In this case, the body simply makes up the lost resting time by going into longer periods of big-wave sleep on the following night. Most people find that a normal period of sleep, that is about 7 to 8 hours, is enough to repair the damage of a late-night party—although it does not take into account other bad effects which might also be present—like alcoholic poisoning from too much drink!

Paradoxical sleep

There is another level of sleep, however, which, because of its 'contradictory' nature, is known as paradoxical sleep. Although the terms 'orthodox' and 'paradoxical' may seem to be an unnecessary complication in the matter of sleeping, it is important to use this distinction. It is easy to make the mistake of thinking that one or the other of the two main stages of sleep is deeper or of better quality. In fact, you should have a fair share of both kinds of sleep for the mind and body to function efficiently.

In the late 1950's, EEG experiments undertaken by Dr. Nathaniel Kleitman achieved a breakthrough in the study of sleep and dreams. It was discovered that people have periods when the wave pattern changes again, this time to a shallow-wave pattern. Their eyes move rapidly about at the same time, up and down and from side to side, although the lids remain closed. You can often notice this kind of reaction in sleeping dogs or cats: their noses or mouths twitch, their tails swish and their eyes seem to be moving, as if looking at something.

This period, called REM (Rapid Eye Movement) sleep, appears to be the time when humans dream most vividly. It would not be true to say it is the only time, for during experiments, people have sometimes been awakened when their eyes were still and their EEG readings showed big-wave sleep, but they were still interrupted in the middle of a dream. However, it does appear that if a person is awakened during REM sleep he remembers his dream most clearly. Georg Mann, a colleague of Dr. Kleitman's, once described the process as being like a visit to the theatre: the sleeper/dreamer sits in his seat, at first fidgeting expectantly. Then he slowly settles down ('alpha wave' sleep) until he seems spellbound by the action on stage (REM sleep)

> 'I was at Hawkwell (a house which we had owned in 1949) and my ex-husband was talking about something which was "up the road". In the dream the road was a different road from the one that really ran past the house and I knew we had never been up it. So I asked him suspiciously what he knew about this road. He admitted sheepishly that he had been looking at a new house which was being built up there, which he rather liked. Without actually moving I could see the unfinished house. I asked him what we would get for our house if we sold it. He replied instantly, "£38,000". I thought, "How the hell did he know that?" I knew somehow that the new house was selling for £27,000. So I said, "Why don't we sell this house and move into the new one?" I don't remember any more.' (NB. The house prices are very specifically in terms of 1970's values, rather than 1949, which seemed to be the period in which the dream took place.)
> Librarian, female, 56

watching everything with his eyes until the curtain falls. Finally, he shifts again as the play ends ('delta' waves).

Studying people asleep in this way has dispelled one very common misconception: that dreams only take a second or two to occur, even though they seem very long to the dreamer. We now know that dreams take exactly as long as the events would take in real life. People who have dreams or nightmares which force them to wake up at night find that they feel terribly low the next day. They have in fact experienced a loss of satisfying sleeping time.

You may think that the time when you dream is the time when you are most 'relaxed', when the mind has all its defences down so that these strange pictures from your private underworld can well up into your brain—but this is not the case. During this kind of sleep, the brain is actually sending messages down to the body muscles to stop any action. The muscles of the body are completely relaxed. Remember the description of the man in the theatre, who sits 'spellbound' by the action. The brain prevents us from acting out the events in the dream world. This discovery has helped to explain the horrible sensation when you want to scream but can't or you try to run but remain rooted to the spot, which characterizes vivid dreams and especially nightmares.

Why you need to sleep and dream

How do we know that sleep is vital? This question is easy to answer: it was common experience during World War II when prisoners were tortured by being kept awake, that after a comparatively short period of time, they would suffer serious personality disorders as well as physical discomfort, and some actually died from the effects of sleep deprivation. The fact that the prisoners were forced to stay awake, rather than being allowed even short periods of sleep, was the worst aspect of the torture. Walking about, prolonged shouting sessions, hot and cold showers —any number of activities had to be maintained to keep them going.

The brain must have its regeneration period of sleep and fights very hard to get it. It is perfectly possible to 'drop off' even for a second or two if you are short of sleep. How often has the rocking of a train or the droning voice of a boring public speaker resulted in your nodding off involuntarily?

A regular rhythm or pulse is a great sleep inducer: the cradle and the rocking chair are domestic proof of that. But strangely enough people fall asleep just as readily through something which ought to be stimulating. They sleep in front of the television or at concerts and plays—and then complain bitterly that they cannot sleep in bed! There is also a danger of accidents or damage in jobs which involve driving long distances or operating machines in a factory. Work does not become easier to do because it is repetitive—it is harder to maintain concentration, and people who work in such conditions cannot help but make mistakes or put themselves at risk. It is part of their human make-up.

Learning in bed

The ability of regular rhythm to induce sleep also counters the science-fiction idea of 'learning in one's sleep'. Many people believe that you can learn a foreign language or the lines of a play by playing a repetitive recording through earphones while you are asleep. It seems unlikely that this could ever happen, since the process of sleep stops the stimulation of the 'wakeful' part of the brain which is normally the area capable of learning and memorizing new information. In fact you are much more likely to be woken up by a recording, just as you would by the telephone or alarm clock.

However, the best time to learn in bed is for a short period when 'alpha rhythms' are present. This is when the body is relaxed ready for sleep but still awake mentally. Perhaps this accounts for the pleasantness of reading in bed—quite complicated material can be well absorbed at this time of night. But don't overdo it—if you're trying to cram for exams or finish vital work for the next day, you'll do more damage by not having enough sleep than forcing yourself to stay awake and learn!

Sleep is vital, in both its orthodox and paradoxical forms, and it follows that dreaming is all important as well. But don't worry if you think you never dream. You do—but you may never *remember* them on waking.

Scientific experiments have shown that if a person is deprived of sleep altogether, then his first night's sleep afterwards will be spent in a greater proportion of orthodox, deep-wave sleep than usual. But after that, on the second or third night, he will make up the paradoxical sleep of vivid dreaming that he has missed. This suggests that both kinds of sleep are equally necessary and work in different ways for our benefit. It might simply be habit to have these two kinds of sleep, but it is also possible that orthodox sleep feeds our body, while paradoxical sleep feeds our mind or brain.

Bad sleepers

It is quite possible that someone who complains of being a 'bad sleeper' might be expecting too much and might be getting quite enough sleep for his own needs. Older people definitely need less sleep—the cells of their bodies and brain are not being renewed at the same rate as a growing child. Remember also that short snatches of sleep—even seconds long—can fall on people, so that in an apparently sleepless night, you can never really be certain that you didn't 'drop off' for a moment. People who sleep badly probably come straight up into full consciousness from deep-

wave sleep more often than 'good' sleepers, who usually have a period of doziness before awakening fully. In other words, bad sleepers remember periods of wakefulness more vividly than other people and consequently believe that they hardly sleep at all.

Sleeping pills

People often believe that sleeping pills will help them to sleep 'well', especially if they are plagued by distressing insomnia. However, there is a great danger in their use, especially the barbiturates. Many psychologists have produced evidence that if you take sleeping pills, you do not get the normal amount of paradoxical sleep—the sleep of vivid dreams and mental regeneration. People frequently find that even though they take sleeping pills, they do not wake up feeling refreshed—a complaint that can now be explained partly by the need for two kinds of sleep.

It may be a temporary relief from the day's worries to force the mind into

Gustav Doré's 'The Exercise Yard' conveys the despair of sleeplessness. Luckily the body has an invincible capacity for snatching sleep.

oblivion with barbiturates. But in the long run, this is only evading the issue. You are actively preventing your mind from facing up to your life-situation and possibly from helping you to understand yourself, so that whatever you are doing can be sorted out. Worse still, as the body really dislikes these drugs, it will make strenuous efforts to overcome their effect. This is what happens when the effect of the drug begins to 'wear off'. It is not uncommon for people to experience far worse sleeplessness and much more intense 'imaginings in the night' than if they had not embarked on pill-taking in the first place.

Sleeping pills can be just as habit forming as alcohol and can have just as serious results. If people would think of them as dangerous, perhaps they would not damage themselves by relying on them habitually.

THE VICTORIA AND ALBERT MUSEUM. LONDON

An interesting sidelight to the problem of drugs can be seen in the immense reaction that many individuals experience after an operation under full anaesthetic. An anaesthetic immobilizes the body, cutting out physical pain and conscious awareness. However, it could be that part of the brain does register what is going on, which is why anaesthetics can give a nastier shock to the system than the surgery performed under it. Even a minor event like having tonsils removed can bring about very vivid dreams for days or weeks afterwards. If one isolated, safely supervised event can have such marked repercussions on the brain, no wonder that prolonged pill-taking is so

destructive, even if at first it seems a dull, wonderful relief.

No-one would suggest, however, that prolonged periods of sleeplessness should be ignored, and no doctor would discuss them as mere complaining. Severe insomnia can be successfully treated—but not merely by popping in a pill every night year after year.

Sleepwalking

Sleepwalking is a severe form of night disturbance, often incorrectly associated with insomnia. It is, on the contrary, linked with the deep orthodox sleep where no eye movements occur. Sleepwalkers are not acting out the

events of their dreams, but the activity seems to indicate that there is some form of mental activity going on in orthodox sleep. People have reported dreams when awakened during this stage, but they are generally less vivid and more difficult to remember for any length of time. The exact nature of the mind's activity during sleepwalking is still a mystery, but it may indicate emotional disturbance. In a child it appears most commonly to be a sign of anxiety or upset, so a doctor should be consulted if it persists. The one excep-

Children are especially prone to visions of 'bogey men' during the dozey phase before sleep.

JOHN FERNLEY

tion to this advice would be if the family had a long history of sleepwalking—for some reason the phenomenon is quite often hereditary.

Things that go bump in the night!

One of the most familiar and easily explicable forms of night disturbance is found during the 'dozey' phase, which takes place just before deep sleep and also just before normal awakening (as opposed to a sharp jolt into alertness). The commonest effect is to imagine that you are falling or that the whole bed is floating. It is also well-known to have a quick imagining of a car crash and literally to jump or start violently at the moment of impact. For children this is the time when 'bogeymen' stand at the foot of the bed, or eerie faces float before the closed eyes. One man remembers vividly that a head made of black and yellow houndstooth check tweed would hover at the end of his bed almost every night at one period of his childhood! Everyone knows the dread of seeing a menacing stranger in the room—it turns out to be the same old dressing gown on the back of the door. The scientific name for an experience of this sort is a 'hypnagogic' dream, a word which only signifies the time when these visions appear, which is in the period leading towards sleep.

All this activity of the brain is reflected in the wave patterns taken from sleepers wired to an EEG machine. Falling asleep is not a steady flow downwards into deep relaxation, but the 'alpha waves' of drowsiness—although regular —rise and fall on a general downward path. It is like watching the flames of a dying fire: they fade steadily, but there can occasionally be a little burst of life.

Dreams and your body

The idea of linking bodily states with the content of dreams is one that has excited great interest for many years. At one time it was thought that dreams were merely the result of eating a heavy meal too late at night. Certain foodstuffs, such as cheese, were supposed to have a particularly strong effect on people, causing vivid dreams. Any form of physical imbalance, such as the discomfort caused to the stomach from over-eating or indigestion, can cause dreaming, but nevertheless does not account for the extraordinary pictures created in our dreams. If food was the reason for a dream, as opposed to one possible cause, people eating cheese would all have exactly the same

cheesey dream—but they don't. However, certain patterns can be noted in the way the body adjusts to outside stimuli. If someone falls asleep resting uncomfortably on an arm, he is quite likely to have a dream involving something unpleasant happening to that limb, such as paralysis or being wounded. But as dreams tend to draw attention to something we should recognize about ourselves, it would be quite feasible that the mind could choose this bizarre way of letting the sleeper know about the discomfort—forcing him to wake up or at least turn over.

In one series of experiments, Calvin Hall, the American researcher, has proved this kind of influence on dreams by placing a waxed candle in a dreamer's hands on two occasions. The first time, the man dreamed he was playing golf, and the second time, he imagined he was lifting weights in a gymnasium! Hearing a tap dripping is a familiar example which often transforms itself in dreams into something like rain, tears, or pouring wine. Sleeping on one's back can cause pressure on the spinal cord and some dreams re-create the pain in a nightmare.

Nightmares

Nightmares are dreams which create a picture or feeling which is so terrifying or disturbing that it wakes you up. Some scientists believe that certain body functions are behind them. Small children find the emotions of rage or hatred so strange and overpowering that at night they re-create them as a particularly forceful dream-picture. This idea is reinforced by the fact that nightmares start in children just about the age when they develop an understanding of good and bad behaviour. So, saying to a 4 or 5 year old, 'You'll really get it if you pinch Suzy again' impresses on the child a sense that many of its natural feelings are bad and dangerous. Consequently he has nightmares in which he realizes the awful consequences of letting 'naughtiness' get out of hand. In older people nightmares can often be a repeat of these childhood fears and may indicate that there is a problem still unsolved in the person's character.

This idea is taken further by other psychologists who believe that people often have nightmares as a result of half-understood physical sensations. Girls in their teens, waking up to the idea of sex, often have very intense dreams which are representations of their emerging sexual drive. What you do not understand often frightens you

—and so the dream becomes a nightmare, with a 'big black thing' chasing you and your legs refusing to move. Dreams of falling from high places can be quite terrifying as well—but they can also occur with no feeling of fear at all! Some of the most disturbing nightmares that adults experience are caused by anxiety. As often as not the events of the dream may seem inocuous enough, but the atmosphere of fear, disgust, anger, sorrow or bewilderment will be the dominant feeling, enough to wake you and leave you feeling disturbed and agitated for some time afterwards.

Dreams and illness

There is an extension to the physiological aspect of dream-making that occurs rarely, but cannot be overlooked. It has been known for someone to dream of being seriously ill, in a very specific way, such as dreaming of suffocation, when in reality the dreamer is a victim of asthma. There are also notable instances of precognitive dreams about illness, in which people have dreamed of having a heart attack or a brain tumour several months before the conditions have actually been diagnosed.

Many people dream about things of which they are afraid or worried, so in most cases a dream about illness will have this simple cause behind it. It expresses the worst fears of the dreamer, so that the problem of anxiety is brought into the open. In rare cases, it could be that the heart trouble or other disorder is present in some slight form, and this registers on the unconscious mind before the conscious one, producing a dream-picture of the trouble. No one should believe that 'bad' news in a dream will necessarily come true: a dream about cancer probably indicates that you have a real anxiety about this illness and the best way to cure that is to have regular checks, as advised by most doctors.

Whatever the factors which cause a dream—outside noises, inside stomach grumblings, or imagined fears—the pictures which are presented to a dreamer are unique, private and endlessly varied. The poet Keats once described sleep as a 'soft embalmer of the still midnight', and asked,
'Save me from curious Conscience, that still lords
Its strength for darkness, burrowing like a mole'.
But research has shown that sleep, while essential and refreshing, still allows the burrowing to continue for our own good.

Dreams without Freud

Dream interpretation is not new; it is one of the oldest and most widespread arts. Ever since man has been capable of coherent communication he has been fascinated by the meaning of the strange frightening and inconsequential meanderings of the unconscious.

The Mesopotamian theory

Of the early civilizations known to man, Mesopotamia developed the most comprehensive and sophisticated explanation for dreams and their language. The emphasis laid on sex by Freud's theories is not as revolutionary as you might think. In ancient texts written by the Babylonians and Assyrians, some dating back as far as 5000 BC, a large amount of space is devoted to explanations of sexual images in dreams.

If a man dreamed that his urine streamed out directly against a wall and spread in the street, then he would have many children. Dreams of flying, which Freud interpreted as symbolic of sexual pleasure, were a subject of great interest to the Mesopotamians. They wrote long books on the various meanings, but most agreed that flight signified danger or death.

These early books about dreams contain many images and symbols of everyday actions, especially eating and drinking, and deal with animals such as donkeys, horses, goats and cats. The Mesopotamians believed that dreams came from evil spirits or demons and that they were like spells, bound to come true unless the dreamer did something to avert them.

The Babylonians had a goddess of dreams, Mamu, to whom they prayed and whose priests performed rituals to stop dreams from being fulfilled.

Nebuchadnezzar's dream

In the Bible, the Babylonian king Nebuchadnezzar dreamed of a strong flourishing tree, cursed by a 'holy one', which turned into a withered stump. The Hebrew prophet Daniel, who was renowned as a dream interpreter, told the King that the image forecast madness. The Bible relates that one year later, Nebuchadnezzar did indeed become insane, 'till his hairs were grown like eagles' feathers, and his nails like birds' claws'. This can be seen either as an example of an evil spirit's dream come true, as the Babylonians would have believed, or as showing that Nebuchadnezzar felt within himself a premonition of his own illness and downfall. Certainly the dream is a good example of the Jungian view that all images are reflections of the self: the tree was the king's mind.

Dreams of the Egyptian dynasties

Egyptian relics of dream books show that their beliefs were quite similar to those of the Babylonians and Assyrians, although they do not date back as far in time—to about 3000 BC. They too were concerned with sexual dreams, and incest and bestiality crop up very often. No one is certain whether this means that people really did make love to their close relatives or to animals, or simply had fantasies about it. The Egyptians subscribed to the theory that dreams come from evil spirits who had to be appeased in some way. However, there were dreams from good spirits, too.

Pharoah's dream

The Old Testament is full of stories about dreams, the best-known being those told by the Pharoah to Joseph. Seven well-fed cattle came out of a river to feed in a meadow, followed by seven lean ones, who then ate the fat cattle. On the following night, Pharoah dreamed of seven good ears of corn that were eaten by seven thin, blasted ears. Joseph interpreted these dreams correctly as a forecast of seven years of plenty to be followed by seven of famine. Notice how the dreams go over the same ground on two consecutive nights, using different images to convey the same message. This trick is still recognized in modern theories as a part of the dream language.

Dream temples—Egyptian style

The Egyptian word for dreaming means the same as 'to keep awake' and shows that they connected dreams with some great state of knowing or seeing things in the dark. So deep was their faith in dream messages that they built temples to which they would go to pray for helpful dreams. Skilled dream-interpreters were on hand to explain the contents next day. If a revealing dream would not come, then there were a host of spells and incantations to make one appear. One remedy was to 'take a cat, black all over, which has been killed; prepare a writing tablet and write with a solution of myrrh the spell and its destination and put it into the mouth of the cat'.

Dreams in ancient Asia

The ancient Chinese and Indian people went much further with their studies of dreams. They did not simply work out lists of what certain images in dreams meant, like the Mesopotamians and Egyptians had done, and they modified the idea that dreams come from outside forces, from good or bad spirits.

The ancient Chinese made a distinction between the different levels of consciousness long before western psychologists began to discuss its existence. They accepted that dreams are produced by the unconscious mind and wrote many books studying the different symbols used in dreams, including the I Ching which is arousing great interest nowadays among people interested in the workings of the mind. Its approach seems to many to have a deeper insight into the subject than many books of western philosophy.

The Chinese rationalization

Chinese writers tried to work out some overall reason for dreams, drawing on astrology and taking note of the time, season and bodily condition of the dreamer. Dreams were classified into several types: ordinary, terrifying, thoughtful, waking, joyful and fearful. (These were mentioned in a book written around 500 BC: the Lio-tzu). Like many ancient peoples, the Chinese believed that in sleep, a part of the body is able to wander, to experience dreams, and that great care must be taken not to rouse the sleeper too suddenly, before he has time to return to himself. Nowadays this idea is still given credence by spiritualists and others who believe in 'astral projection', the idea that everyone has an 'astral body' capable of leaving the physical one and wandering at will, usually during sleep.

This quaint medieval view of Nebuchadnezzar's dream shows the effects of his later madness. His dream was a classic example of the subconscious revealing death or a future illness.

Indian understanding

The idea of different states in the body intrigued the Indians, who also developed a subtle understanding of different levels of consciousness. They thought there were four states: waking, dreaming, dreamless sleep, and a fourth, which is a mystical union with the god Brahmin. It is extraordinary to think that several centuries before Christ, the notion of distinction between different types of sleep was already being considered, although it has taken years for modern scientific research to confirm this with EEG machine experiments.

One of the earliest Indian dream books is contained in the Atharva Veda, an old collection of writings dating from around 1500-1000 BC. Among its many fascinating ideas is the suggestion that if a man has a series of dreams, only the last should be considered important. This ties in neatly with the modern concept that several dreams work through a problem in different ways until they find a solution. The Indian theory suggests that they realized that dreams could have a purpose.

They also accepted two kinds of imagery in dreams: those relating to common experience and those having a more general wide symbolism. This is a feature of modern understanding that finds echoes in the early writings. Images which Freud took to be sexual—swords, axes, flags—were taken to mean happiness. Symbols such as the sun or moon falling from the sky or dreams involving the sea or mountains suggested messages of a different kind, usually dangerous or fearful. This is rather like Jung's explanation of archetypal images, which people everywhere can recognize, whatever their own personal experience. Basic emotions are expressed through them.

Perhaps even more remarkable insight is found in these early Hindu writings in the practice of looking at the temperament or character of the dreamer. This was only hinted: the main drift of ancient Indian belief was to think of some mysterious 'other force' at work, but nevertheless, even a suggestion that someone's personality is related to his dreams is a very modern idea.

The Classical idea

Fundamentally, the eastern religions of Hinduism and Buddhism are much more contemplative than those of the western world, so perhaps the emphasis on states of mind is understandable. In comparison, the classical worlds of Greece and Rome used dreams more as signs about how to act or what was going to happen. Famous writers and poets such as Homer give many instances of people prompted to action because of some message from a god revealed in a dream.

Dream temples, Greek style

The hero Achilles in the story of the fall of Troy, the Iliad, believes that the god Zeus will aid the Greeks with advice revealed in a dream. So widespread was this view that the Greeks took up the Egyptian idea of building temples where people could go to sleep, to dream and to have a 'divine' message descend on them.

The temples were dedicated to Aesculapius, the Greek god of healing, for it was also believed that medical cures could be achieved through dreams. A dream could specify the right kind of treatment, besides revealing to someone a proper course of action. Hippocrates, (a medical man from whom we still have the 'Hippocratic oath' which doctors are supposed to swear) wrote a book about dreams, one of the few that have survived from the classical era.

The Hippocratic theory

Hippocrates explains in great detail a belief shared by the Greek people with other parts of the early world. Everything that happens to a human being, in sickness or in dreams for instance, is a reflection of some larger state of affairs in the universe. A man is controlled by the powers that cause the sun and moon to shine or the earth to bear crops, and so an event like an eclipse or a flood has

a terrifying effect. It also explains why the idea of some outside power or god speaking in dreams would have been credible.

The Platonic theory

Not all Greek thinkers shared this view. Plato developed an explanation of dreams that bears some resemblance to Freud's line of thought. At night, he said, we have a 'wild beast' roaming around inside us, while reason sleeps. The passions in us which drive us to commit murder, sacrilege or incest can come out in dreams. Freud also narrowed down the kind of drives that make us dream to those of sex and power. There is a noticeable link in his theory of the conscious and the unconscious with Plato's idea of reason being asleep while the wild beast roams.

Dreams and Romans

The Romans held to most of the views of the Greeks and were prompted by their dream images to do things with just as much sincerity. Hannibal crossed the Alps after being encouraged in a dream, and Julius Caesar came to power in the same way. When returning to Rome at the head of his army, he dreamed one night of sleeping with his mother. This he took as a sign of 'entering the mother land' and promptly crossed the Rubicon into Roman territory with his troops. This entry was forbidden unless a general disbanded his forces first and was symbolic of seizing the power of the empire.

Artemidorus: linking past and present

The most famous of all books about dreams to come out of the classical world was written by Artemidorus of Daldis in the second century AD. Throughout his life, he gathered together a vast store of ancient documents relating to dreams in order to write a major study of the subject. He actually used material from the great library of the Babylonian king, Asurnasi at Nineveh. In this way, a clear tradition of dream interpretation survived from the earliest days of civilization to the first centuries of the Christian era. Perhaps these strange connections account for the disrepute which fell on Artemidorus: he was taken up by magicians and quacks seeking to prove some mystical line of authority back to ancient prophets and seers. But if all this is left aside, the real value of Artemidorus' work is immense. He was the first person to see clearly that dreams are made up of a number of

images, strung together in a sequence. He believed it was very important to study the whole dream and to see the images in their setting. This has long since been accepted as an essential method for worthwhile understanding of dreams. Second, Artemidorus said that it was always necessary to have a good knowledge of a dreamer's personality and his life situation—and that is exactly what modern psychoanalysts try to discover and what you should apply to the interpretation of your own dreams.

'I was riding down the road on a bicycle and somebody started following me, also on a bicycle. He started terrorizing me — I was terribly frightened and I kept trying to get help, but I could not speak or shout. All the time my hands kept getting caught in the spokes of the bicycle wheel.

I got to a phone booth and two traffic wardens walked by laughing and talking and they saw me struggling and screaming trying to get into this telephone booth but I could not actually get anything out of my throat at all, and they obviously were thinking "How cute, this young couple you know, having a lark", and that frightened me even more. Eventually I got in the phone booth and I tried to telephone Mike, my husband, to save me, and then I realized that he was the one who was terrorizing me at the same time. Eventually I actually managed to get the words out and I actually shot up in bed screaming for help.'
Picture researcher, 25, female

There is more than a grain of truth in another suggestion from Artemidorus: many dream images have a strong sexual element, he said. The plough in the furrow, the horse and carriage and the granary store were all studied in what we now call 'Freudian' terms. He also commented, 'a mirror means a woman to a man and a man to a woman', which neatly expresses the same idea as Jung's description of the Animus and Anima. These two are our sexual opposites, acting as an expression of our aggressive, masculine nature or passive, more feminine side.

CHRIS YATES

Muslim dream theory

Dream interpretation began to go out of favour in Europe once the magical associations surrounding Artemidorus' theories became known. Only the non-Christians, the Muslim Arabs, continued to be fascinated by it.

They studied all the writers from classical times and from the far eastern part of their empire, where information filtered through from China and the Indian sub-continent. Subtle and mysterious explanations were put forward, and hundreds of books, from dictionaries and encyclopedias to religious treatises and magical poems, were written by Arab scholars.

Mahomet's explanation of faith

Mahomet, the founder of Islam, used dreams as a way of explaining the faith. He relates in the Koran a dream in which the angel Gabriel takes him on a journey through the night, riding a silvery grey mare, all the way to Jerusalem and then up to heaven. He meets Adam, the four Apostles, Jesus and finally sees the Garden of Delights. He meets God, who gives him instructions for his people about how many times a day his people should say their prayers. Then the beautiful grey mare

flies through the dark sky, back to the spot on earth where he had fallen asleep.

Although there were many knowledgeable dream interpreters, the Muslims tended to explain dreams in a way that fitted in well with their religious beliefs. And there are some amazing insights in Arabic works:

'He whose soul is pure is never deceived by his dreams, whereas he whose soul is blemished is continually deluded'.

There also was an attempt to understand symbols, especially those which we now consider to be Jungian archetypes. But in the end, the skill was limited by the main purpose, that of explaining people's thoughts in terms of the rules of the Islamic faith.

Dreams and Christianity

In the Christian world, dreams fared even worse. The Church frowned on 'interpreting', believing it was involved with sorcery and black magic. It only allowed the possibility that dreams could be divinely inspired. It is very interesting to see that all the dreams reported by religious figures in the New Testament and in early Christianity do not require any interpreting at all. They are nearly always straightforward mes-

Mahomet used his dream of a journey to heaven on a silvery grey mare to inspire faith, but it could be seen as an expression of his own ambitions as a spiritual leader.

sages of encouragement from God. There was no thought of foretelling a man's future, for that was in God's hands.

Francis of Assisi

St. Francis of Assisi recorded many dreams which he had at important moments in his life, all of which gave him the strength to carry on in his life of poverty and to continue the establishment of his order of Franciscan monks. One striking image came to him just before a very difficult interview with Pope Innocent III. He saw a tall tree with wide, thick branches before him. As he looked at it in admiration, he felt himself growing and growing until he was the same height as the tree. He touched it with his hand and it gently gave way, bending down at his touch. St. Francis saw this as a sign from God that the Catholic Pope would give way and accept his ideas. (Notice how both St. Francis and King Nebuchadnezzar took the world-wide symbol of a tree to express their wishes and fears.)

51

Famous precognitive dreams

This limitation on dream interpretation continued for many centuries, and only in the last hundred years have people begun to look at dreams from the point of view of the personality. The other aspect of their contents that fascinated thinkers was the occurrence of dreams that seemed to foretell the future.

Nearly all biographies of famous people contain such startling incidents.

Francis Bacon, Elizabethan writer and scientist was staying in Paris while his father was lying seriously ill in London, England. One night when his father was near death, Bacon dreamed of his family home in the country, and that it was plastered with 'black mortar'. This led him to believe that there could be some form of telepathic communication between blood relatives.

Oliver Cromwell when a young man had a dream in which a huge female figure drew back the curtains round his bed and told him that one day he would be the greatest man in England. Cromwell especially noted later that no mention had been made of the word, king. (The female figure could be interpreted as the Jungian concept of the anima: while Cromwell's remark could be a good example of 'secondary revision' as Freud would say – adding in a conscious detail to an unconscious experience.)

Queen Marie Antoinette, overthrown and imprisoned by the French revolutionaries, had a dream of a glowing red sun rising above a column, like a temple pillar. Suddenly the column cracked in half and fell to the ground. Her image has been understood to represent the fall of a powerful figure.

Shelley had a dream no less than a fortnight before he drowned in the Mediterranean, sailing from Leghorn, in

which friends came into his bedroom, seriously wounded and bloodstained, with staring faces, warning him that the house was being flooded by the sea. He also dreamed in the same moment of strangling his friend, Williams, who did indeed drown with him.

Charles Dickens had a dream in which he saw a lady in a red shawl with her back towards him. She turned round and introduced herself with the words 'I am Miss Napier'. Dickens had no idea who this person was, but the very next night, after giving one of his famous readings, some friends came backstage, bringing with them the selfsame woman, and introducing her as 'Miss Napier' in real life.

Bismarck, the iron ruler of nineteenth century Germany, dreamed of the rise to power of Prussia over the other German states. This actually came true and was one cause of the First World War.

Abraham Lincoln dreamed of his own violent death, with his body lying in state on a catafalque.

Adolf Hitler had a most extraordinary dream as a young man during the First World War. He was a member of the German Infantry and found himself in the trenches on the French front. One night, he dreamed of being buried beneath an avalanche of earth and molten iron and of being severely wounded. He woke up and felt compelled to leave the trench in spite of warnings from his comrades. No sooner had he started to scramble away from the dug-out than a fearful explosion thudded behind him. Hitler turned back to see the trench completely collapsed and all the soldiers dying under a mass of earth and hot metal. It has been said that the event encouraged Hitler to believe that he could not fail in his plan to dominate Europe.

Nowadays, a large part of dream research is directed into this area of dreams which foresee. Sometimes of course it can be argued that they are merely another version of wish-fulfilling or problem-solving dreams. Both Marie Antoinette and Bismarck might be expected to have such dreams, given the circumstances of their lives. But not all, certainly not Hitler's dream, could be brushed off in this way.

Lord Tennyson dreamed of Prince Albert coming to see him and kissing him on the cheek. 'Very kind but very German' he said to himself in the dream. The very next day, he got a letter from Windsor Castle informing him that he was to be Poet Laureate.

The Duke of Portland, who was involved in arranging the Coronation of Edward VII, had a dream that the king's coach got stuck in the Arch at Horse Guards on its way to Westminster Abbey. Although the State Coach had been used before, he insisted on the arch and the coach being measured, and found that the top of the coach was too high to pass under the arch. Since its last appearance, the road surface had been raised due to repair work, and everyone had overlooked the fact.

Dreams in primitive cultures

These are the traditional views and mysteries of dream history. Now that you have seen how many ideas date back to the earliest civilizations, you will not be surprised to learn that psychologists have gathered some very useful information in recent years from looking at present-day primitive tribes, some nearly extinct. The data collected can yield valuable comparisons and sidelights on the way that all minds work, primitive or sophisticated, and shows how widespread and fundamental certain ideas are.

The Siriono of the Amazon
Looking at tribes all over the world has proved that people dream to a large extent about the everyday facts of their lives, wherever they are. We might have dreams situated in houses and motor cars, whereas the Siriono natives of the Amazon in South America dream about

hunting in the jungle. Just as we use the image of the car to suggest other things besides transport, (mechanical emotions, sexual drive and so on) so the Siriono people dream about hunting, even when they are not hungry. They turn hunting into an image to suggest other things. This leads to the conclusion that all human beings use typical parts of their living pattern to make images in their dream world.

The Sioux Indians
Many discoveries about so-called primitive people suggest that perhaps they have better ways of living than we do ourselves! The North American Sioux Indians, for example, dealt very kindly with the misfits of their society. They somehow fitted them in, instead of shutting them away in a kind of institution. They did not regard the criminal, the insane or inadequate as shameful or

stupid. They put all the blame on evil spirits who had infected the dream world of these poor people and treated them as best they could. In a way, this recognizes that people have an unconscious part to their minds that produces drives without respect to the conscious part. Other tribes seem to have understood this too, although it took western civilization many centuries to come to the same conclusion through psychology.

The Iroquois Indians
The Iroquois Indians worked out a theory that dreams may say one thing

In primitive societies, the barrier between the world of dreams and ordinary daily experience is not so sharply defined. The Sioux bear dance was a symbolic enactment of the roles of hunter and hunted.

but mean another, and they devised special techniques to help people discover the true meaning. The Iroquois used a method rather like that suggested earlier of writing down or recording all the thoughts that spring to mind in association with a dream image to build up some impression of what it represents.

Once the Iroquois dreamer had a clear idea of what wish was being expressed or what problem was being confronted, then the Indians would 'make it come true' by acting it out, either in reality by staging an argument or in a ritualistic way. More developed societies also have ways of releasing some urges as a ritual — all the howling and shouting at a football game could be viewed as a fairly healthy way to express aggression!

The Hurons

The Huron Indians had a theory which has quite noticeable resemblances with modern ideas about dreams. Like many primitive cultures, these Indians believed that the 'voice' of the dream world was a guardian spirit, which gave revelatory messages, but in disguised form. These could be warnings about enemies, disclosures of special cures for diseases or good advice about the best places to go hunting. Especially interesting is the belief that this 'spirit-voice' could reveal the hidden wishes of the scul – rather like the Freudian idea that dreams are expressions of unconscious urges or wishes. The Hurons came even closer to modern thought when they suggested that perhaps the 'spirit' or 'soul' inside is made happy or satisfied by expressing its desire in dream form. This led them to wonder whether in fact physical illness or emotional upset is caused by the 'spirit' rebelling because its desires are not recognized – not far off present-day thinking about psychosomatic illness.

The Diegueno Indians

These Indians of Southern California have been studied with great interest because they devised a technique of psychotherapy through dreams – a development not found very often among primitive people. The 'treatment' was confined to people who were suffering from a particular type of obsession or fantasy. This was sexual and consisted of excessive dreaming on the subject, in mild form, or hallucinations, when it was considered serious. These visions would be of a 'spirit-lover' plaguing the sufferer. The treat-

ment would be to have a lengthy conversation with a shaman or magic man, who encouraged the patient to confess his fantasies and discuss why they are so absorbing. The shaman declares that he might as well tell all, because he knows all about it anyway, through his magic powers. He might also recommend the sufferer to go on a special healthful diet – or get married! But the significant aspect of this Diegueno custom is that the remedy takes the form of a consultation – a talking-out with an expert – much the same as a modern analyst works. In most primitive groups, remedies are usually more physical: people 'act out' the dream or dance away the affliction.

> Two recurring dreams:
> 'I'm in some play or other, but I've been idle about learning my lines. I've lost my script so I search high and low, but I can't find it and no one else will lend me one. Then it's time to go on stage, and I still don't know my lines.'
> Librarian, female, 56
>
> 'I kept dreaming that I was going down a spiral staircase — like in a castle or church tower, As I went down it got narrower and narrower until I was stuck with my shoulders above and my legs round the corner below!'
> Housewife, 30

The Ashanti People

The foregoing examples concern American people, but of course, African studies have come up with equally varied and surprising facts. These too help to build up some basic conclusions about the nature of dreaming, worldwide. The Ashanti of West Africa, for example, had also caught hold of the idea that dreams can mean exactly the opposite of their apparent content, just as Freud has pointed out in his Interpretation of Dreams.

To give an example: someone may dream that a hunter kills an elephant. The Ashanti method would be to look beyond the immediate images and find the real answer by association of ideas. The elephant is the most powerful animal of the jungle, so he must represent a king or chief. The Ashanti would

say therefore that the dream is a warning that a chief will die in the near future. A similar explanation is given for a dream of a house without a roof. This is a symbol foretelling death because for the Ashanti, spirit people live in a world of roofless dwellings.

The Ashanti also share the common idea that the 'voice' of a man's dream is a spirit, and they believe that it can be someone's ancestor speaking. It is a widespread notion, and takes many forms. With the Ashanti, the ancestor often appears in dreams in animal shape. Some anthropologists have been led by this idea into linking dreams of ancestors with totem worship. This is simply another way of saying that primitive people maintain a strong sense of their tradition and identity by worshipping their ancestors and by personifying them as animal or half-imaginary beings. This sometimes involves making actual totem images of them, which are respected and revered by the whole tribe.

Totems and dreams

There are many different theories about what totems are, but the basic idea explained above is common to several of them. A totem acts as a symbol of the group or tribal identity and is often imbued with magical or beneficial powers. This story from a Canadian tribe reveals how totems work for primitive people: A man went out hunting and met a black bear who took him home and taught him many things. After a long stay with the bear the man returned home. At first he looked and acted so like a bear that everyone was afraid of him, but someone rubbed him with magical herbs and he became a man again. After that, whenever he went hunting, the bear helped him catch his quarry. The man built a home and painted a bear on it and his sister made a blanket with a bear design too. Then all the descendants of his sister used the bear crest and were always known as the bear clan.

Such legends occur all over the world and very often the origin of the totem comes from a dream picture. Totems can be personal too: among some Australian aborigines, witch doctors adopt a special totem after dreaming of a particular thing, such as a lizard or a kangaroo. A rather attractive custom from the Dyaks of Borneo illustrates

The most striking characteristic in dreaming among African cultures such as the Ashanti is their belief that dreams are as real as waking experience.

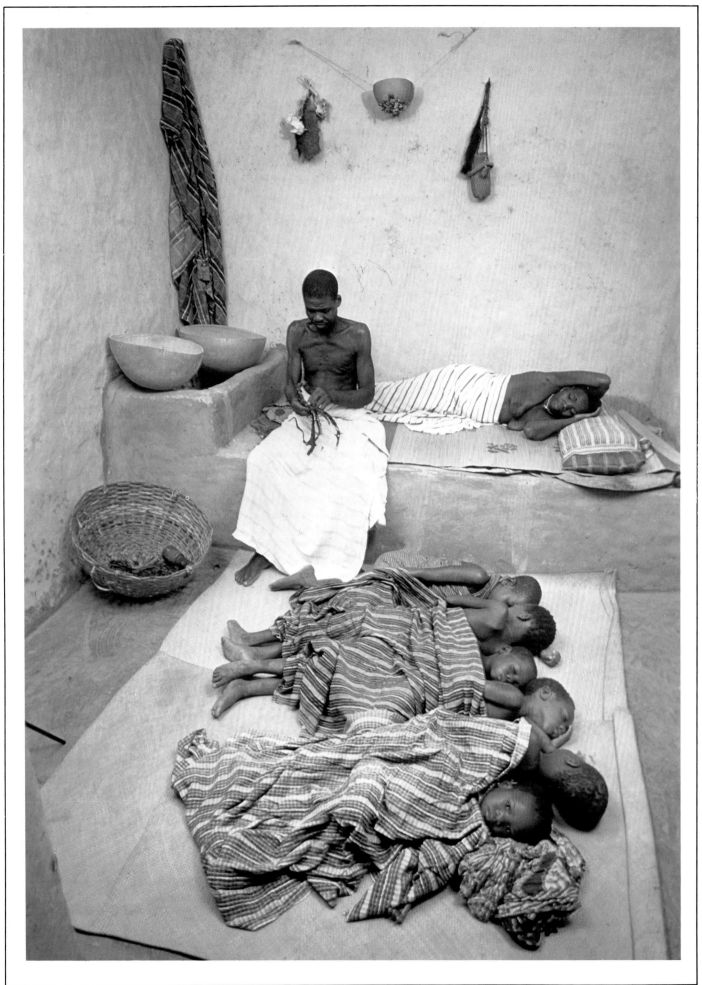

55

how far and wide this dream influence extends: if a man dreams that something of value is given to him, then when he wakes, he picks up the first curious object he sees – perhaps a shiny stone on the ground. He takes it home and hangs it over his bed, and when he next goes to sleep, he addresses it and says he wants a dream with good pictures about some matter or business which is important to him at the time. If he has such a dream he keeps the object and it becomes valuable to him, but if the dream is unhelpful he throws it away and waits for another such opportunity.

Dreams directing reality

It is quite common among primitive people for special talents or careers to be marked out by a dream experience. Among the Blackfoot Indians of North America for instance a man became a medicine man after he had had a series of dreams in which a dead relative came to him and gave him detailed instructions on how to work cures or cast spells. In many tribes, a young man who intends to become a priest can only do so if he has a dream of making contact with a god first. This is a reminder of the Old Testament story of Samuel, who as a child heard a voice in the night and thought it was his priest, Eli. But the priest, who had been sound asleep, realized that the boy had heard the voice of God.

General conclusions

It seems that primitive people have two kinds of dreams: those that relate to their own personal situation and which come to them quite spontaneously, or those that are more important, containing messages or visions about the whole life of the tribe, its identity and importance. This second kind is sometimes called a 'culture' dream and is obviously considered valuable. In many tribes, special customs exist to induce this kind of dream. They help to keep the group sense of security and well-being, or they can result from the dreamer's wish to be blessed by his ancestors or receive good omens from the 'spirit' of the tribe. In our own culture, we have examples of this kind of dreaming, like Joseph's dreams, and their importance in Bible history.

Dreams are used by primitive people for a number of other social functions, like choosing a person's career or guiding his work. In fact, primitive people use dreams in ways not far removed from those which present-day interpreters

suggest they are considered for problem-solving and help towards better self-understanding.

'True' dreaming

The most general belief that characterizes primitive people's dreaming life is that at times they can be just as real and 'truthful' as everyday life. There are endless variations on this theme. If an Ashanti dreams of adultery then this

> "I'm in London and for some time without explanation, the streets have been getting sinister splits in them and steam and smoke start oozing out. Men with wheelbarrows of tar keep trying to fill the cracks. Nobody talks about it but every time you go past a street that's been newly tarred, you know that's another one where the steam has got through.
> I go to visit a friend on the other side of London, in a room with a few large plants, a hickory floor, Bauhaus furniture. We decide we had better get out of London. We run as fast as we can go to Victoria Station. There's a bus like an airport bus, with no seats in it, only some ill-fitting, garishly patterned carpet. A thick, bull-necked man with an SS armband comes up and says "You haven't been members of the Party. You can't leave London."
> We start running, running back to my home, and everywhere the streets are cracking open, melting, boiling, and the smoke is so thick it's dark as night. We rush into a black marbled doorway where there are electric lights and luscious green plants with red and orange veins.
> Then the lights go out and flames start creeping out of the crevasses."
> Magazine editor, 36.

results in his paying a fine just as if he had committed the act. The Didinga people of the south-east Sudan had the custom that if a man dreamed of another as a victim of witchcraft, then the dreamer had to go and see him the very next morning and avert the evil by a series of elaborate ritual acts. If a member of the Dyaks of Borneo dreams

of falling into water, he believes that this has actually happened to his spirit and so has to summon a shaman or priest-figure. The shaman 'fishes' for the lost spirit in a basin of water with a little hand net until he catches it and returns it safely to its owner. A tribe in Brazil called the Bororo once deserted a whole village in a panic because one of them dreamed that he saw enemies approaching on the attack. But perhaps the most famous anecdote on this subject comes from the distinguished pioneer scholar in anthropology, Levy-Bruhl, who wrote how a chief in equatorial Africa had a dream that he travelled to Portugal and England. When he got up the next day he put on European clothing and announced his journey to his friends, who all gathered round and congratulated him on his wonderful luck!

The power of dreams

Primitive people may use dreams to predict the future or direct the actions of the tribe or clan. Or they can use dreams to sort out some personality problem, or even a physical illness. The interest for us lies in seeing how primitive people believe so absolutely in the power of dreams. It is easy to see that if a young man dreams that he is in contact with a god, for instance, and accepts this as a message that he should become a priest, then probably it is his own desire or motive that brings about the dream. The curious thing is to note that if a tribal custom requires a dream of this sort, then it will occur.

Old and new

Some anthropologists are specializing in studying primitive people whose lives are being radically altered by contact with the outside world. In some cases, people seem to adjust quite well and incorporate Western ideas into their dream patterns, alongside the old beliefs and customs. This could provide an interesting application of dream study. It might help to show if a group was acclimatizing to the new way of life at a fundamental level or whether their adaptation was only successful to the casual outside observer. The strain of coping with a new culture, a new way of living and thinking, could be detected through changes in their dream pictures.

Many primitive peoples chose their totem or clan symbol from dream images, which in turn were usually drawn from the natural world around them – animals, birds, trees, the sun, moon and stars are often featured in this way.

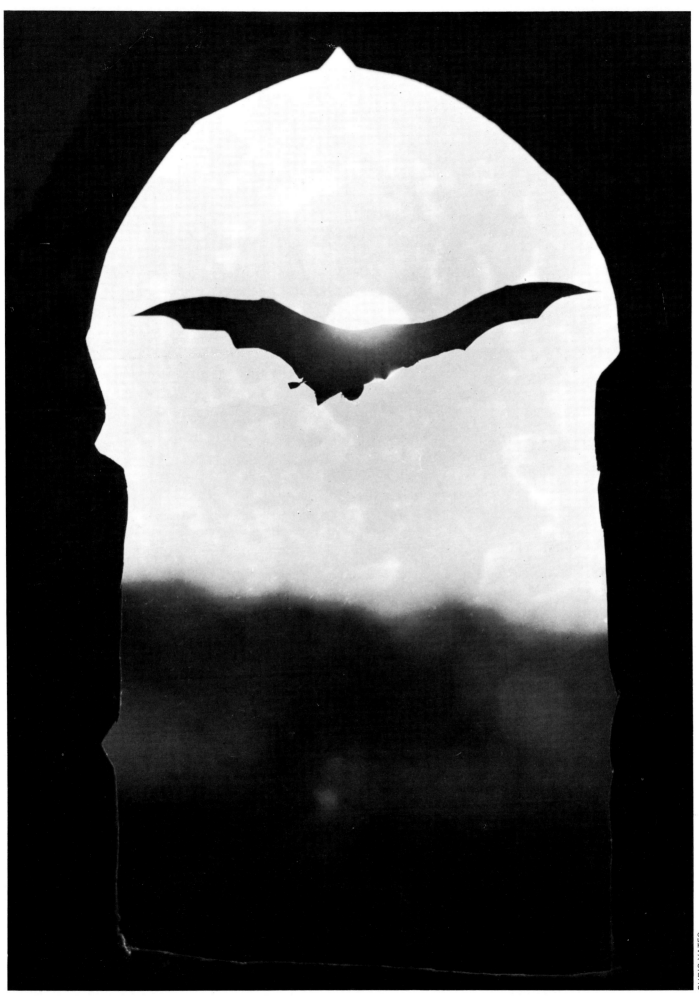

57

Only a dream?

You may have come to the conclusion by this stage that you can read just about anything you like into a dream and interpret it in at least a dozen different ways! Of course you have to weigh up the possibilities in an image. Is it a symbol? Is it an image for something of a sexual or other nature? What did you feel about these images at the time of dreaming, and what do you feel now, thinking about it?

The chances are that there will be some overlapping between your answers, especially if you are getting close to the purpose of the dream. If you construct a 'theory' about a dream, you will immediately know inside yourself whether it is rubbish or not. But you will find that you cannot impose an idea like 'reversal' or 'displacement' on any old dream and come up with an answer. When you feel a little click in your head, or a lurch in your stomach and a voice saying 'That's it!', you will have no doubts about it. Dream interpretation only has real value if you recognize and accept the truth for yourself.

Inspiration while they slept

Through the centuries, man has used dreams in most remarkable ways to enrich his life. A wide range of achievements have been made possible through these bizarre sleep experiences. You can learn something of yourself and, if you are lucky, about the world outside.

In sleep when the mind is sifting information and the input of data is reduced, there is a greater chance of putting two and two together.

Archimedes leaping out of the bath shouting 'Eureka!' is a story everyone knows—he had suddenly worked out the secret of measuring the volume of solids by their displacement of water. In a lovely state of slumbering relaxation, with no effort from his conscious mind, he hit upon the answer to a problem which had occupied him for weeks and months.

Niehls Bohr, the famous Danish physicist, offers a more up-to-date example. When he was a student, he had an extraordinarily clear dream of a sun composed of burning gas, round which planets were spinning, attached by thin filaments. He awoke to realize that this dream image showed the structure of the atom which gave him the inspiration for further research into atomic physics. However, these flights of inspiration do not always involve such abstract scientific concepts.

Elias Howe was an American who wanted to design a really practical sewing machine. He dreamed that he was captured by savages and ordered by their king to produce a perfect sewing machine—or else! He tried and tried, but without success. His fate approached: the savages advanced raising their spears to kill him.

Suddenly Elias noticed that all the spears had eye-shaped holes in their tips. He awoke with a start and realized that the dream had uncovered the secret for which he had been searching: the thread on a machine should go through a needle hole near the tip in order to run smoothly. A small detail, but it revolutionized the design of sewing machines.

Friedrich Kekule's was probably the most well-known dream discovery. He hit upon the exact shape of the so-called 'benzene ring'—the atomic structure of the benzene molecule—with a dream image of a snake swallowing its tail. The instantaneous and accurate nature of this discovery led him to say to a group of scientists in a speech: 'Let us learn to dream, gentlemen, and then we may perhaps learn the truth'.

Thomas Edison, the inventor of the telephone, was so sure of the value of dreams that he developed the habit of snatching forty winks between hours of work and believed that a great number of his best thoughts and inventions came to him in these drowsing moments. (He was also a great believer in ESP.)

Of course, these kinds of experiences also happen to people in waking life: a flash of intuition, a sudden moment of truth is as much the way of scientific discovery as slow plodding progress. But what fascinates experts is that during a dream, which is supposed to be a jumble of images from the unconscious mind, a real insight into the workings of the world can so often be revealed.

Dreams and art

Not only in the realm of science, but in art too, dreams have their part to play.

Freud once said that it was not himself, but the poets who 'discovered the unconscious'. Throughout history, art and literature have been greatly enriched by the fantasies that have stirred in creative minds.

Shakespeare often described dreams through his characters, as a reflection of their state of mind. Lady Macbeth is a dramatic portrayal of a mind haunted by guilt: a clear image of hand-washing represents her desire to wash away her sin. In *Richard III*, the king has a tormenting dream before the battle of Bosworth—as if his unconscious is forcing him to see the tragic, drastic consequences of his lust for power. Shakespeare rightly suggests that King Richard's fear lies within himself—in the conflict between his urge for power and the pain that such destruction brings him.

Wordsworth wrote many poems as a result of dream visions—he once said that he felt he had 'lived in a dream'.

Coleridge's poem *Kubla Khan* was dream induced, although the poet also took drugs, which may have affected his imaginings.

Novelists have often found their plots and characters through dreams.

Jules Verne's *Twenty Thousand Leagues Under the Sea* certainly explores that dark underlife populated by Jungian archetypal creatures, monsters of all shapes and sizes.

Charlotte Bronte used dreams to great effect in her classic novel of childhood, *Jane Eyre*. Through the little girl's dream images, the author conveys better than any other words could express the loneliness, fear, and frustration of her life:

'A feeling as if I had a frightful nightmare, and seeing before me a terrible red glare, crossed with thick black bars. I heard voices too, speaking with a hollow sound, and as if muffled by a rush of wind or water: agitation, uncertainty, and an all-predominating sense of terror confused my faculties.' This is an authentic and vivid description of a typical childhood terror which perhaps Charlotte Brontë experienced herself, to be able to use it so well in her book.

Edvard Munch's Anxiety *captures the blank dread which must have clouded much of his own dreamworld.*

59

The Surrealists

After Freud's theories were first published, many artists began to dwell on the idea of the unconscious mind and thought that they too should invesigate this new way of looking at the personality. The paintings of the Surrealist movement perhaps capture the peculiar style of dreams better than any other school or generation of artists. Surrealism really began in France in the 1920s. It was defined by one of its founders, the writer André Breton, as an attempt to create art from the mind's eye, to express the real functioning of the mind 'in the absence of all control exercised by reason'. Breton wondered, as many dream theoreticians have, 'Couldn't the dream be applied to solving the fundamental questions of life?'

In capturing dream visions in paint, the Surrealists have helped people to recognize the amazing depth and richness of the unconscious mind. Their work has made people realize that there are many different kinds of 'reality' besides the one we see in during waking hours. Surrealism attempts to reach a new awareness, to lead to a better harmony between the conscious rational mind and unconscious forces. The word itself means 'over-real', a new level of consciousness, with the two levels of the mind better integrated.

Celluloid dreams

The Surrealists did not only use paintings to explore this possibility. Many of them realized the great flexibility of the motion picture to express it—notably the French writer Jean Cocteau and film directors René Clair from France and Luis Buñuel from Spain. Buñuel is still making brilliant surrealist films, superbly adapted to modern ideas. Many other film directors have played with the distinctive characteristics of dreams to convey the working of the mind very successfully. Early examples of 'dreamy' films were mostly confined to movie-fantasies, just as many dreams are pure wish-fulfilment. Women sighed over Rudolph Valentino or Clark Gable, men over Loretta Young or Jean Harlow, and the expression 'dreamboat' for handsome men is still around. But later directors began to look more deeply into the style of dreams.

The dislocation of events in dreams can be perfectly captured on film. Among the best are Alain Resnais' *Last Year in Marienbad*, Fellini's *8½* and *Juliet of the Spirits*, Antonioni's *Blow Up* and Ingmar Bergman's *Wild Strawberries*. Not just 'intellectual continentals' can do it—consider *2001: A Space Odyssey*, *Yellow Submarine*, *Barbarella* or *A Clockwork Orange*. They all have sequences that perfectly convey that mad, floating 'alternative reality' of dream experiences. Audiences have become so adjusted to this film technique now that if a person suddenly moves from one place to another—say from smiling at a child to seeing her run over, as in *Sunday, Bloody Sunday*—they know it means that the first is what is happening, while the second is what is being thought at the same split second. The essential feature of dream

Salvador Dali's 'Impressions of Africa' is a striking example of the Surrealist attempt to capture the 'other reality' of dreams.

SALVADOR DALI

technique in films is that so far it has only tried to imitate the way minds work during sleep. A whole new movement in the arts is trying to break down the barriers between consciously imitating and actually releasing this unconscious working of the mind through hallucinogenic drugs. The dangers behind this kind of experiment are obvious. But some people find the results so overwhelming, so startling and original however that they are prepared to take the risk. The feeling of 'breaking down the walls of the mind' was strikingly captured in the final sequence of *2001*—other examples can be seen in *Performance* or *Easy Rider*.

It's easy to see the continuing preoccupation with the 'freewheeling' processes of the mind in the 'pop' culture of today, whether the images are stimulated artificially or not. Look at the LP covers in any local record shop and you'll soon see that many have designs or photographs which draw heavily on strange juxtapositions, weird landscapes and representations of the archetypal symbols and images of all schools of dream interpretation.

Present-day research

Many psychologists believe that the brain acts as a filter, hindering our perception of 'supernatural reality', shown to some extent in dreams and the effects of hallucinogenic drugs. Present-day research is moving more and more into this realm of 'another reality'. But no one really knows the full extent of the mind's powers. Are those midnight inspirations nothing more than freak occurrences, or could dreams be used to release more knowledge? This whole area is usually termed 'psychic research' and means investigation into 'paranormal phenomena' which are not totally explicable by the present laws of science. Until fairly recently, this field of the paranormal was regarded in a dubious light, only attractive to eccentric old ladies and deluded gentlemen who liked to dabble in the occult. But now it is gaining ground as an area for serious work, and no wonder, with an overwhelming mass of well-authenticated evidence waiting to be studied.

Foreseeing the future

One of the main areas of study is precognition in dreams—those hundreds of cases where people have foreseen events during sleep. A typical incident comes from the novelist J. B. Priestley. He had a vivid dream in the 1920s of sitting in the front row of a balcony,

FOX-RANK

M.G.M.

looking out across some dimly-seen, majestic and colourful spectacle. More than ten years later, he found himself visiting the Grand Canyon in the United States. The canyon was covered in a thick early morning mist and as it cleared, the vast, impressive Colorado landscape spread out before him. At once, Priestly recognized it as the identical place of his dream.

There are countless cases of people reading newspaper headlines in a dream announcing an earthquake or similar disaster before it occurs or at the same time, and during the First and Second World Wars mothers frequently dreamed of their sons being

Top: Buñuel's film 'The Discreet Charm of the Bourgeoisie' incorporates a common dream situation: the fear of sudden exposure. Below: the park sequence in 'Blow Up' by Antonioni brilliantly conveys the 'other sinister reality' of narrative dreams.

killed, as the event was happening.

It is possible to pass off a sizable proportion of these 'precognitive' dreams with a simple explanation. If a person wakes up for instance 'knowing' that something has gone wrong, it may be that his mind has an acutely developed sense of awareness that comes through even in sleep to give a warning in

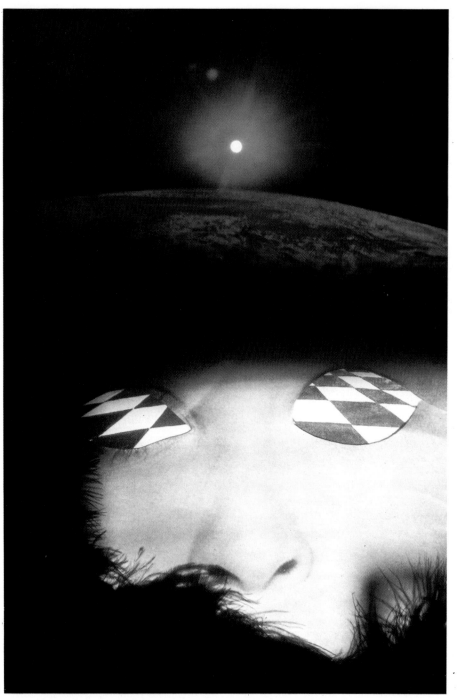
CHRIS YATES

extreme situations. This would account for those miraculous escapes from falling bombs or avalanches. Many other incidents are simply the result of worry and coincidence.

But the inexplicable dreams, foreseeing incidents that are quite beyond likelihood or visualized in such detail that they are genuinely 'psychic', pose much deeper questions. It could be that the movement of time as we know it is only one way of arranging events. Perhaps incidents in the future can 'be known' before they happen. Even more peculiar, can we know about the extreme past in great detail?

Reliving the past
Dreams about someone else's past life,

Even the most bizarre images that appear in dreams could contain a hidden meaning for the dreamer.

including names and places, have been alleged and have attracted a great deal of interest. One man could recall a previous existence as a naval gunner at the time of Napoleon and came up with such accurate details that Earl Mountbatten used the material as evidence while discussing naval history with experts. A woman called Mrs Smith seemed to recall the entire life situation of a girl who lived in 13th century Toulouse in dreams, visions and a kind of half-automatic writing. As in the case of J. B. Priestley, Mrs Smith recognized parts of her dreams on a holiday visit.

Dream communication

A theory that is being slowly accepted is that everyone has some degree of extra-sensory perception, or 'ESP'. At its simplest level, this means that you might be able to receive information from other people by a kind of invisible radio, without knowing them—and without even intending to. This would explain dreams relating incidents from the past or simultaneous events across a physical barrier, such as the problems of a relative overseas. But the real 'future' dreams are still a mystery.

Some fascinating experiments in this field have been undertaken recently by two American doctors, Montague Ullman and Stanley Krippner. They have been trying to show that in a dreaming state, people have more powers of telepathy or ESP than they do when awake. Usually these powers are associated with psychically sensitive people, but it could be that in sleep the faculty to perceive things in this way becomes much more widespread.

The experiments usually took the form of having an 'agent' who concentrated on a particular picture or idea and tried to get it across to a sleeping person, or 'subject'. The subject's dream would often incorporate the picture or idea being transmitted. The doctors learned to refine this phenomenon. Just as most ordinary dreams are concerned with people and problems, the best transmitted pictures or ideas were those dealing with these themes. So if an agent concentrated upon a picture of eating, drinking or a beautiful woman, then a male subject would be very likely to dream in a clear way of the subject matter.

How accurate are the results? In one example, the agent was looking at a painting by Monet called 'Corn Poppies'—in it a field of flowers forms the background and a woman walks across the foreground with a child. The subject's dream that night included plants, a lady 'dressed up' and a child. Now of all the things that the sleeper could have dreamed, such exact parallels with the agent's 'message' are remarkable. Multiplied by hundreds of similar tests, the results of Ullman and Krippner's experiments lead to some striking conclusions.

Nightmares could be a transmission of someone else's horrifying real-life experience. Incidents in the past might contain such powerful human emotions that they live on and get 'picked up' by another mind, even hundreds of years later. Perhaps we might even learn to develop this faculty usefully.

KIM SAYER

Leave your dreams to chance

The whole question of 'chance' may have to be re-examined in the future, if dream research continues to explore in this direction. How often have you come across some extraordinary coincidence: you dream of a friend you haven't seen in years, and the next day a letter from that same person arrives in the morning post. Normally you would dismiss this as a once-in-a-million occurrence. Now, as psychic research increases available information it seems that chance occurrences may actually be 'willed' by the unconscious.

Everyone must have experienced the terror of being chased in a nightmare: could this be the transmission of someone else's horrifying experience in life?

Interestingly, as well as exploring the unconscious mind in their paintings, the Surrealists also adopted chance methods of achieving their ends. Anything that came together on the canvas, as if by accident, might perhaps hold some unconscious meaning. The artist Paul Klee once said that his aim was to 'make chance essential'. In the light of these ideas, that is not as absurd as it sounds.

What is fortune telling?

Fortune telling falls into two parts: the divining of the future and the reading of character and how it has been shaped by events in the past. Palmistry alone combines both of these facets — the other methods in this book are concerned solely with one or the other. This book can be used in several different ways — for serious attempts to read character or the future; for fun and entertainment among friends, or simply for the curiosity value of a collection of past beliefs. There are sections which fall into each of these categories. Numerology uses the logic of mathematics to bring order out of apparent chaos. Palm reading and phrenology — the reading of lumps on the head — can be amusing to try out on friends and the collection of past beliefs — the meanings of moles, for

example — and the section on tea-leaf reading, make fascinating reading.

Methods

Since time immemorial man has tried to give Fate an opportunity to make its intentions known by using the operations of Chance. And it is from these that all methods of foretelling the future developed. Some are no longer seriously used; some, however, many people take very seriously. I Ching, one of the oldest methods, has many devoted adherents, and the Tarot pack continues to draw believers. Perhaps it is the more obscure and complicated methods which inspire faith. The pack of cards used in everyday life to play poker, patience or snap has no longer the same aura. We find it difficult to

believe it can reveal our future. But the Tarot — its signs and figures clearly fixed in the remote past — we feel can tell us something. It is as though Fate, being mysterious, needs a mysterious vessel to work through.

In the following pages there are fortune telling methods both old and new. All of them are interesting and fun to use even if you do not place much faith in some of them.

Character

If you can tell fortunes or reveal character you will find that people gather around like bees after honey, clamouring to be told about themselves and their character. And this is one sure way to get conversation going at a party! A further dimension is added to your self-knowledge when your character is told. If the fortune teller is on target there is the surprise of having your views of yourself reinforced or modified or your self-deceptions shattered.

The fascination lies in the fact that things you thought were only known to you are suddenly revealed as apparent to others too. And this is revealed objectively. It is not simply other people's views of your character which happen to coincide with your own. The fortune teller has divined them from an outside source, whether cards, a palm print or the lumps on your head. And even the sceptic can be somewhat unnerved by accuracy obtained like this without rational provision of data.

Yet this is not so strange; finger prints are accepted as unique (they are used regularly in the detection of criminals), so why should not the same apply to palm prints? It could be that what is unique to you might in some way reveal something of your inner self.

The future

The future is fascinating to everyone. You frequently consider the past and remember how often you have been overtaken by surprise, how many opportunities you missed because they presented themselves too suddenly, how may offers of help you spurned because you misunderstood them. 'If only I'd known', you murmur.

As a result even the most sceptical people keep some corner of the mind free for an unacknowledged hope that perhaps, in some way, such knowledge just might be obtainable. There the mind allows itself to accept omens, superstitions, portents and the telling of fortunes. And even if you don't actually believe implicitly in these it is possible that alternative courses of action may be indicated which had not previously occurred to you. You might even consider acting upon them.

On the other hand, if you believe in an underlying pattern in events, that the seeds of the future lie in the present, then you believe in Fate.

Some methods of telling character can be claimed to be scientific because they relate directly to the subject rather than the operations of chance working through cards, say, or tea leaves.

Phrenology, on the other hand, started with scientific pretensions and has now largely fallen into disrepute. But it remains amusing, and a good party game guaranteed to claim the attention of the person whose lumps you are reading.

Telling your own fortune

You can attempt to peer into your own future by using cards or the I Ching. In general, however, fortune telling demands a 'diviner' and a 'client'. This is because you cannot stand far enough away from yourself to interpret your own future without bending the facts slightly to suit your wishes.

Learning by heart?

It is, of course, better if you can memorize the meanings of the cards — both ordinary and Tarot — tea-leaf formations and so forth. If you do then there will be no hesitations in your readings, no searching through this book for the relevant passage!

On the other hand, you can simply familiarize yourself with the meanings and then refer to the text as necessary. This can be an even more impressive method. Friends and acquaintances might mistrust your reading if they think you are using your imagination rather freely. But they will probably tend to believe and accept your predictions if they see you referring to a text and then interpreting it. Interpretation is, perhaps, the most important factor in fortune telling so the need to refer back to the book does not detract too much from your impact or your claim to be a fortune teller.

Be responsible

Beware when reading other people's futures. Many people, however much they protest disbelief, will half believe or be disturbed by any prognostications of doom and disaster that you may give. Use your tact and discretion in deciding how much to reveal, and when. If reading futures or characters in public — at a party, say — be careful. Your client may be secretly pleased to hear he will change his life, go abroad or marry three times — but his wife may not be.

Intuition and imagination

When you reveal the character or tell the fortunes of others your intuition, sympathy and awareness all come into play. Fortune telling when done face to face depends largely on the interaction of minds. Mutual sympathy is important. If you the fortune teller are responsive to and aware of the client's reactions, the reading has a better chance of success. Let your subconscious and imagination have full rein. Many of us are more intuitive than we think and if you temporarily discard logical thought processes you may be surprised at your own powers of discernment.

At the simplest level fortune telling can be an amusing party trick and a very good way of getting to know people. It can also offer clues to greater self-knowledge and a chance to glimpse future possibilities.

The language of signs

Long before writing was invented, man used a rich vocabulary of signs to express hopes and fears about his own life and the world that surrounded him.

The five pointed star is one of the most ancient signs — certainly older than writing. It was believed to be a protection against witches.

Three arrows bound together — a sign of unity.

A sign used to cast out evil spirits.

SNARK INTERNATIONAL

Omens, oracles and signs

There is hardly anything which moves which has not at one time served as an omen, hardly any human activity which was not surrounded with its own superstitions. The direction a bed faced has been thought significant — for riches, the head should be to the East, for a long life, to the South. Money was supposed to come to you if you sneezed to the right, good news if you dropped and smashed an egg or had a shoelace which kept coming undone.

Fortune might attend you if you picked up a pin, met the same person twice on the same journey or broke uncoloured glass (but if that glass was a mirror or a bottle then bad luck would follow). The sight of bellows and the burning of bones was once considered unlucky. If you wanted to avoid evil fortune you had, apparently, to not cut your hair before the new moon, avoid meeting grave-diggers, be careful never to cross two forks or two knives, and not mend clothes while you were wearing them. You should also never — unless you wanted to tempt fate — put your left shoe on before your right, break a pair of scissors, sit on a table without keeping one foot on the ground and, of course, never open an umbrella indoors.

It is as though everyone felt they were on the verge of disaster all the time, kept from ill-fortune only by a series of inconsequential yet desperately important actions. At any moment one might unknowingly trigger off disaster. The spilling of salt, the breaking of a plate, even a sneeze — especially, it seems, on a Monday or Friday — could summon bad luck which had been lying in wait. If one believed all this then every action, every occurrence became an oracular pronouncement. All that was necessary was to know the appropriate meaning and one was then forewarned and prepared for what the future held in store.

Omens

People believed that Fate was constantly active and, therefore, that every-thing which occurred had a fateful message to convey. Every passing cloud, bird or breeze, every accident of nature, became part of the code by which one's future fate could be reveal-ed so men scanned the earth and sky for omens.

Even now sometimes you probably catch yourself out not walking under a ladder, feeling slightly worried about breaking a mirror or waiting for the second magpie to appear. It is not necessarily that you believe in such omens, just that having heard them from childhood there is a vague feeling that perhaps you might, after all, be tempting fate. And people who do disregard them — walking deliberately under every ladder they see — often do so with a certain air of defiance!

However, whether or not you choose to believe in them, certain events and phenomena have, over the centuries, been given particular meanings. Some of the better-known ones are given below.

Animals

Carrying their unconscious forecasts of a good or a disastrous future, these too were thought to be the innocent messengers of Fate.

Bat Bad luck, especially if it cries while flying.

Cat There is doubt about the significance of this mysterious beast. Black, it may be good or bad; experience would have to tell. But to kill one is thought to be disastrous, and if one unaccountably leaves your house, it could mean catastrophe.

Dog Much less involved with fortune telling, but an omen of death if it howls at the moon, although it offers no precise warning of where death intends to strike.

Goat Good luck.

Hare Unfortunate, especially if one crosses your path.

These charming animal drawings are taken from a medieval manuscript. Even today country dwellers still think of animals as harbingers of fate.

Hedgehog Good fortune, especially if met going in the opposite direction.

Horse Piebald, a good omen. (If seen tail first, however, a friend may meet misfortune.) A white horse seen by lovers will bring them good luck.

Mouse White or brown, it means happiness, especially in love; grey, danger threatens.

Pig A bad omen, especially if met immediately after marriage.

Rat Good, if white; bad, if black.

Sheep In a flock, good fortune, especially if approaching.

Squirrel Happiness will be found soon after seeing one.

Birds

Because the flight of birds is so unpredictable, yet so apparently purposeful, their appearance has often been taken as a portent of good or evil fortune.

Crow A bad omen, especially if seen to the left.

Cuckoo Not seen, but heard, it foretells prosperity, especially if it is heard to the right.

Dove A happy omen, particularly for those about to marry.

Gull Settling on a ship, a happy sign for those about to sail in her. But to be touched by a gull in flight is said to foretell the death of someone close.

Hawk Be watchful — powerful enemies threaten. (This is supposed to be especially true if the bird is seen to the left.)

Kingfisher A scandal threatens.

Magpie One, especially on the left, is an omen of death. Two, however, are very lucky and signify that good fortune will follow within three days.

Owl Always bad luck. If it hoots three times, be especially careful.

Robin Good luck.

Sparrow Bad luck, except for lovers.

Swallow Very good fortune, especially early in Spring. If they build under your roof, good will follow. If you kill one, expect disaster.

Wagtail Fortunate, especially if approaching from the left.

Wren Good luck. (But at your peril either harm or frighten it.)

Insects

Their movements are difficult to forecast and their purposes obscure. Perhaps for this reason insects have always been taken to be messengers of Fate.

Ants A nest near your home is a good augury, but to be bitten by one means quarrels and strife.

Bee Good luck if it is trapped for a while in the house.

Cockroach If seen in an unusual place, it foretells a death.

Cricket Always and everywhere thought of as lucky. But if they suddenly abandon a house where they have been settled, disaster follows.

Grasshopper A journey, and good news.

Ladybird A good omen, especially if it has seven spots on its back.

Spider A doom-laden creature: seen in the morning, it means grief; at noon anxiety; in the evening, financial loss. A spider spinning a web means people are plotting. To kill one brings misfortune. However, if found on the body it is a harbinger of prosperity.

Wasp To be stung by a wasp indicates danger, probably through jealousy.

Patterns and shapes

As the patterns made by tea-leaves offer an irresistible temptation to look into the future so, too, did other apparently random formations. These were read in the same way as a tea-cup (see later for the meaning of the symbols). As with reading tea-leaves, it took some imagination and a great deal of concentration to understand the message offered by the symbols!

Egg whites
Take an egg, separate the white from the yolk, and pour the white into a bowl almost brimful of water. After 24 hours, clots will have formed which you should then be able to read.

Sealing wax
Heat a little sealing wax in a serving spoon or ladle. When it is melted, pour the wax into a bowl of clean water. The shapes that the wax forms will give you symbols which contain the answer you need.

Seeds
To discover the order in which certain events will occur, plant a seed for each event — but never enquire about more than five things. Put each seed in a separate pot. As far as possible give each pot the same amount of sunshine and water. The order in which the seedlings appear will give you the information you want. This process is likely to be somewhat lengthy so it is best not to enquire about events in the immediate future.

Simple questions

Several different methods were developed to answer questions which require only a simple affirmative or negative.

Burning paper
Write out a wish or a question on a slip of paper, place it face down on a plate and light it with a match. If all the paper is burnt, you will get what you want. But if only a part of it burns, though your wish may eventually be granted, this will not be for some time.

Cat's paw
If you have a cat, it too can give you a yes-or-no reply. Think of your question, then call your pet. If the right forepaw appears first around the door, the answer to your question is Yes.

Paper pieces
Write a different question on each of a number of pieces of paper (usually thirteen) and then place all the slips at the bottom of a bowl. Pour water into the bowl and wait for the first slip of paper to rise to the surface. The answer to the question on it will be Yes.

Paper squares
Cut two squares of paper, both the same size, and colour one black. Drop them both at the same time from an upstairs window. If the white one lands first, the answer is Yes.

Stones
Fill a wide bowl with water and murmur a question aloud as you drop a small stone into it. Count the ripples in the water — if the number is odd, the answer will be Yes.

Wedding ring
Tie a length of black thread around a gold wedding ring. Hold the other end of the thread in your left hand and then lower the ring into a glass of water. If it touches the right side of the glass then the answer to your question is Yes. If it touches the left, No. If it touches the side either nearest you or furthest away, you may take it that the oracle refuses to answer and should not be consulted for another 24 hours.

Itches

If one believes that all things have a meaning, then even a sudden irritation which demands to be scratched might be able to enlighten you in some way about your future. The message can be precisely deciphered by the place on the body where it has settled. Next time you have an itch, consider the significance it might have.

Top of head Promotion.

Right cheek Someone is slandering you.

Left cheek Someone is complimenting you.

Right eye You will meet an old friend.

Left eye Disappointment awaits.

Inside nose Problems, grief.

Outside nose The saying is 'Kissed, cursed or meet with a fool', this to take place within the hour.

Lips Someone insults you behind your back.

Back of neck A relative will fall ill.

Right shoulder Legacy.

Left shoulder Sorrow.

Right elbow Goods news.

Left elbow Bad news.

Right palm Money comes your way.

Left palm Bills come your way.

Back Disappointment.

Stomach Invitation.

Loins Reconciliation.

Thighs A move.

Right knee Happy voyage.

Left knee Voyage beset with difficulty.

Shins An unpleasant surprise.

Ankles Marriage and/or a rise.

Sole (right foot) A journey with profit.

Sole (left foot) A journey which brings a loss.

Moles

Because one is born with these curious marks upon the body they were often thought significant. The essential information which they give depends

The position of significant moles on different parts of the body.

upon where the moles are placed. The bigger the mole, the more emphatically the attributes and fortunes it foretells will come into being. There are general points to watch for, too, because the shape of the mole has its importance. The rounder it is the more good fortune is implied. If the mole is raised, that means very good fortune indeed; an oval or pointed mole means bad luck, made even worse if its colour is dark, and worse again if it is hairy.

Forehead Right: intelligence, leading to fame and prosperity. Left: extravagance, fecklessness.

Eye Near the outer corner of either eye, placidity of temperament, frugality and thriftiness.

Eyebrow Right: happy and probably early marriage. Left: difficult marriage.

Ear Recklessness.

Cheek Right: happiness, especially in marriage. Left: difficulties, struggles.

Chin Success, prosperity, good fortune.

Mouth Happy, sensual disposition.

Jaw Bad health.

Nose Great fortune, travel, a developed sexuality.

Throat Rich marriage; ambitions attained.

Neck Many ups and downs, unexpected legacies, early set-backs but ultimate success.

Hand Natural ability, leading to success.

Arm Right: success. Left: financial anxiety.

Shoulder Hard and difficult times.

Breast Right: ups and downs of fortune. Left: in a man — fortune and happiness, in a woman — ardent temperament, sometimes leading to foolish attachments. Centre: adequate income, but no great wealth.

Abdomen A nature selfish and self-indulgent, lazy and perhaps greedy.

Back Frankness and generosity, but also arrogance and self-display. If very low: sensuality and self-indulgence.

Ribs Right: cowardice, indolence, insensitivity, boorishness. Left: the same, but less so and modified by humour.

Hips Strong, healthy children and numerous grandchildren.

Thigh Right: warmth of temperament, wealth, happiness in marriage. Left: loneliness, loss, poverty, although the temperament is equally warm.

Knee Right: ease in marriage and with finances. Left: rashness.

Ankle Refinement, leading in a man to dandyism. In a woman a sign of energy and hard work.

Foot Right: love of travelling. Left: swift intelligence.

Leg Right or left: laziness.

The trial of destiny

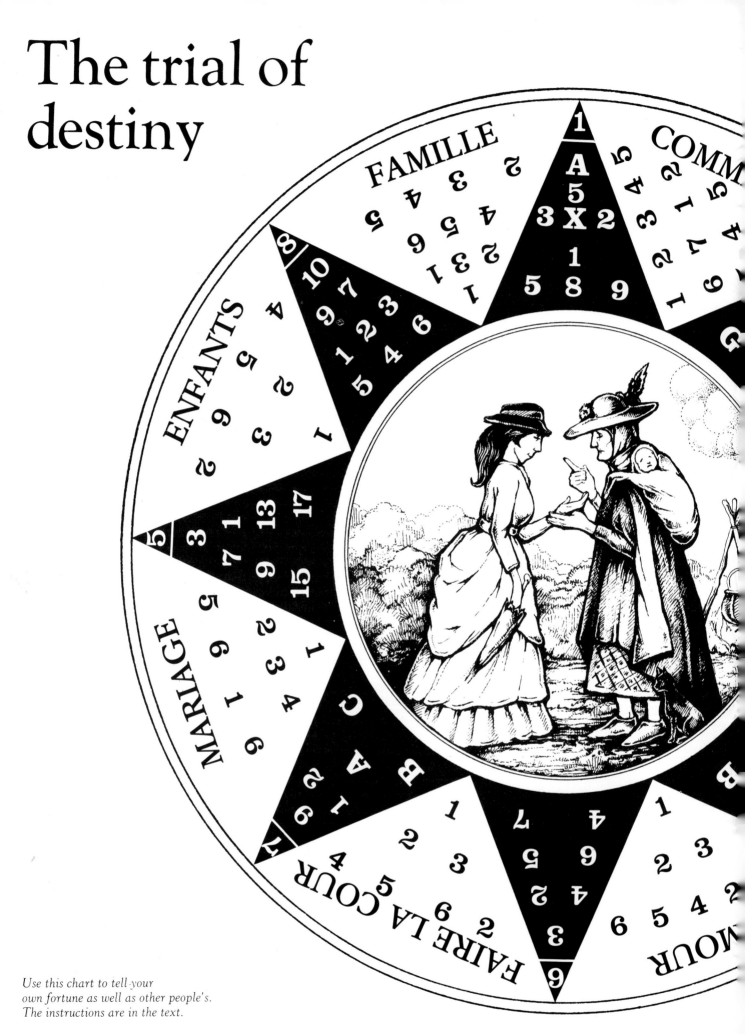

Use this chart to tell your
own fortune as well as other people's.
The instructions are in the text.

Choose which subject you want to ask a question about — you can, if you like ask a question on each subject. Then take a pin, close your eyes and prick the pin into the section of your choice. The number the pin lands on gives the answer to your question. The inner point sections give a general indication of something about to happen to you — and here again you can choose a section. Close your eyes and proceed in the same way. If the pin fails to hit a number, fate is unwilling to answer your query.

Love
1. Many lovers.
2. One sincere lover, one false one.
3. A flirtation.
4. A senseless jest.
5. A lover who has not the courage to speak his mind.
6. You love and are not beloved again, — so banish the flame.

Courtship
1. The lover is sincere.
2. No wedlock is intended.
3. They are wavering in love.
4. A long courtship, to end in nothing.
5. It will end in marriage.
6. A sudden break.

Marriage
1. Happy, and of long duration.
2. Short, but prosperous and peaceful.
3. Not so soon as you expect, but happy in itself.
4. Not so happy in the end as the beginning promises.
5. A separation or divorce before death.
6. A paradise on earth awaits you in this respect.

Children
1. They will surround your table like olive-branches.
2. Several in number, — some as roses to you, and some will prove thorns.
3. One at most.
4. Not many.
5. One amongst your children will raise you to affluence, — they will all prove acceptable.
6. Illegitimate children will trouble you, yet perhaps not your own.

Kin
1. They will enrich you.
2. They will improverish you.
3. They will exalt you.
4. They will degrade you.
5. Some of your kindred will leave you a valuable remembrance.
6. A death in the family.

Trade
1. You will never be indebted to it in your own person.
2. You will suddenly embark on it.
3. You will form a friendship with a trader.
4. You will lose by trade.
5. You will enter into partnership.
6. You will get rich by commerce.

Fortune
1. Changes every seven years will occur to you.
2. A steady life.
3. Sudden riches.
4. Fatal extravagance.
5. False promises will undo your peace.
6. A sudden fall and a great rise will mark your life.

Speculation
1. Success in the lottery.
2. Never speculate.
3. Chance luck.
4. Fortunate at cards.
5. You will be lucky at ventures in trade.
6. Luck in a wager to come.

The points
A a letter.
B a reproof.
C a loss.
D a gain.
E new appeal.
F a gift.
G a journey.
X a disappointment.
Y a feast.

1. A comfortable hour.
2. A change.
3. Bad news.
4. Good tidings.
5. A voyage.
6. A present of money.
7. A valentine.
8. A gift to wear.
9. A present for which you will pay dear.
10. You have lately practised some unworthy deception.
12. A period of anxiety.
13. Moment inauspicious. Try again.
15. You will soon lose something good by passion.
17. A long walk on a sudden occasion — try again. A cross betokens great joy — try once more.

Know that these points only refer to minor affairs, and such as will be speedily verified.

The reading of tea cups

The sediment in the cup one drinks from has in the past often been thought to provide clues to the drinker's fate, because it involves both the random and the personal.

Many people once thought that only those with 'psychic powers' could read cups. But no one has ever been able to define precisely what these powers are. You just may, whether consciously or not, possess them so do not let such a doctrine put you off. With knowledge and practice you may arrive at levels of perception which surprise you. This is by no means a precise science, however, and if you attempt it you will need to exercise your imagination and let your mind wander freely. Learning the meanings will not be enough.

Method

There are one or two basic points to remember. First, use a cup which can be easily read: one that is plain, and not straight-sided. Second, avoid a dusty tea. China tea is supposed to be the best, but any large-leaved mixture will do. (You can, of course, follow exactly the same procedure to read coffee grounds.) To provide the necessary personal link it is also thought to be vital that the subject actually drinks the cup of tea or coffee. In order to obtain the pictures you need, let your client drink almost the whole cup and then swill the remaining teaspoonful around a few times. (Some people insist on a ritual element in this

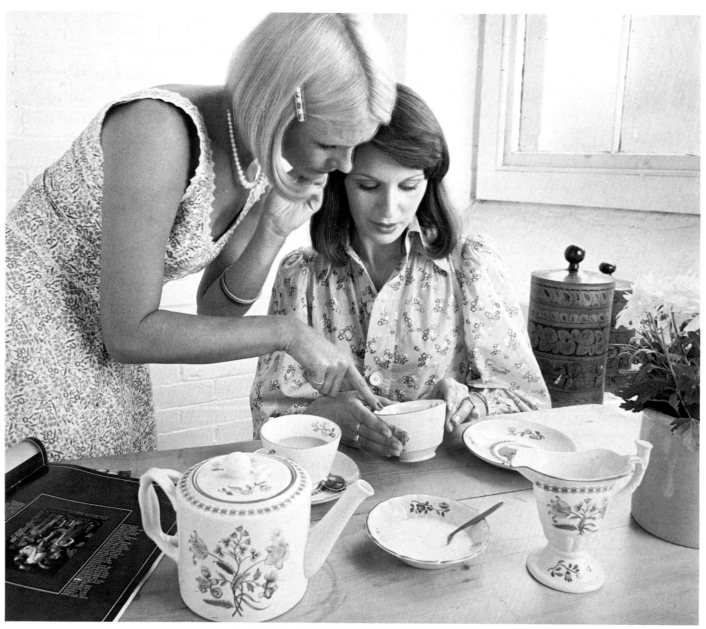

swirling of the dregs, and say it must be done only with the left hand and either three or seven times.)

Next turn the cup upside down on its saucer. When the final drop of tea has drained away, turn the cup the right way up again and begin your reading. Do not hurry. Give your imagination a chance to work. Turn the cup, tilt it, consider it from every angle. The clearer a symbol appears, the greater its importance. Do not, however, expect the images ever to be totally clear. Sometimes the leaves offer no more than a suggestion and it is up to you to interpret such hints. If you really cannot discern any pattern or symbol, tell your client the truth. Although you may allow yourself to add that the confusion of the leaves probably mirrors the state of mind.

Reading the symbols

The meaning of the various symbols is the most important thing. The list that follows gives some of the most commonly used, but your own imagination and, in time, experience, may lead you to add more of your own. The position and size of the symbols are also significant.

The client
The cup-handle represents the client. If a symbol is near the handle it indicates an occurrence close to the person's home. The direction taken by symbols which suggest movement is also important. Some will point to the handle, suggesting approach; and some away, suggesting departure. There is also one theory that, when holding the cup with the handle towards you, symbols to the left of the handle concern events in the past and those on the right events in the future.

Time
The sides of the cup, from rim to bottom, are taken as a time scale. Thus the position of the symbols is important: *near the rim* — they indicate events which will occur in the near future, *near the bottom* — events distant in time, *in the bottom* — ill-fortune at any time.

Proportion
The size of the symbol is also important, for example, the proportions of the symbol will give some indication of the size of the house your client might move to or the legacy he might receive.

Overall reading

First, consider which kind of symbols predominate and make a general assessment of good or bad fortune. This will give a logical structure to your reading. It will tell you whether any bad news the cup foretells will be no more than a minor blemish on a period of happiness, or whether the good will only lighten a bad period.

Remember that the message lies in the combination of all the symbols. Only when you have put them together will what they have to tell become clear.

If an ant and an eye, pointing to perseverance and watchfulness, are combined with a large and very clear gun near the cup's handle, this suggests that it is in the domestic arena that these qualities will be best deployed. If, however, the third symbol is a broken necklace, then the problems through which one has to persevere and over which one must watch arise from a love relationship. And an open book would translate the same effort into the legal field.

Every combination of signs has a different significance, making reading from cups a fairly exacting business, but also a rewarding one.

Left: This seems to be the cup of an unmarried person, for the horse's head on the right suggests that there is a lover in the offing — possibly a rich lover. Yet the head faces away, and that is not a good sign. There may be danger of a swift parting. Opposite the handle there stands a swaddled baby, indicative of a multiplicity of small worries, and the arrow-head which suggests that bad news is impending.

To the left, the signs indicate that a bad time has been passed through: a flying bat, pointing to the plots of false friends: the square, implying unwelcome restriction, and the jester's head which tells us that this situation was taken very seriously indeed.

Right: A period of domestic happiness has come to an end. In the past, to the left of the handle one finds the fish, a symbol of happiness, and a table, suggesting meetings, dinner parties and all manner of pleasant gatherings. But to the right of the handle, danger threatens: a hand grasps a gun, the muzzle toward the cup handle — domestic bliss is threatened, and very determinedly, by an outsider. (A gun can also indicate a call to arms.) Terror follows, for a devil-tailed monster leaps up from the disaster-cluttered bottom of the cup.

Meanings of the symbols

Acorns
An excellent symbol. The good fortune it foretells varies according to its position in the cup:
near the top — financial success
towards the middle — good health
near the bottom — improvement either in health or finances

Aircraft
A sudden journey, unexpected and not without risk
alternatively there will be a rise to new heights
if the aircraft seems broken — danger threatens, either physically or in one's career

Alligator
Treachery lies in wait

Anchor
Success awaits. Again the position in the cup is important:
at the top of the cup — success in business, augmented by the support of a faithful love
towards the middle — a voyage ending in prosperity (increased if dots surround the symbol)
at the bottom — good fortune socially. If the symbol is obscured — anticipate difficulties

Ant
With perseverance, success will arrive

Arc
Ill health threatens either career or other plans, projects may be abandoned, accidents threaten

Arrow
Bad news is on the way

Axe
Difficulties face you, especially if only the axe-head appears

Baby
Many small worries threaten
alternatively, there may be an addition to the family

Bag
A trap awaits, likely to be successful if the bag is closed

Ball
Variable fortunes await you in life

Basket
A very good sign. Again pay attention to its position:
near the handle — a baby will soon be announced
near the top of the cup — your possessions will be added to
if flowers lie in the basket — a very good sign, suggesting happiness, social success, parties and festivities
if the basket is surrounded by dots — finances will be unexpectedly augmented, perhaps by a legacy

Bat
Beware of plots and of false friends

Bear
Irrational decisions will bring difficulties and even danger in their train
if the bear is turned away from the handle a long journey is indicated

Bed
if neat — a tidy mind
if disordered — an undisciplined mind which leads to problems

Bee
Success, both social and financial; good news
near the handle — a gathering of friends
a swarm of bees — possible success with an audience

Bell
News is expected, good or bad according to the significance of the surrounding symbols
near the top of the cup — promotion
near the bottom of the cup — sad news
two bells — great joy

Bird
This is particularly lucky if there are two or more birds
flying birds — good news
standing birds — a successful voyage

Boat
Refuge in time of trouble

Book
If the book is open expect litigation, if closed difficult researches

Boot
Protection from pain
pointing away from the handle sudden removal, perhaps dismissal
broken — failure and disgrace threaten

Bottle
Take care of health

Bridge
Opportunity to be seized for short-cut to success

Broom
Small worries disappear

Butterfly
Frivolous but innocent pleasure
if surrounded by dots this indicates the frittering away of wealth

Cabbage
Jealousy entails complications

Candle
Helpfulness, zeal for education

Castle
Strong character, rising to position of authority

Cat
Someone lies in treacherous ambush, probably a false friend

Chair
Improvement and, if the chair is surrounded by dots, financial improvement

Circle
A successful outcome

Clock
Avoid delay and hesitation
alternatively — recovery from illness
in the bottom of the cup — a death

Clouds
Doubts, unsolved problems
if the clouds are very heavy, misfortune is indicated

Column
Success. Also a danger of resultant arrogance

Comet
A visitor from overseas

Cross
Suffering, sacrifice, tribulation. Two crosses indicate severe illness or other major affliction

Crown
Great success
If the crown is neat expect a legacy

Dagger
Impetuosity
alternatively — the dangerous plotting of enemies

Dog
Rely on friends
Pay attention to the position and attitude of the dog:
running — good news and happy meetings
subdued — you may be slandering a friend
at the bottom of the cup — a friend is in trouble

Dot
A single dot emphasizes the meaning of the symbol it is nearest to. Dots in groups indicate money

Drum
Scandal and gossip threaten. Quarrels are in the air.

Egg
Prosperity, success, fertility. The more eggs the better

Elephant
Wisdom, strength and slow, but solid, success

Eye
Take care and be watchful, especially in business

Feather
Instability and lack of concentration

Fence
Limitation imposed on plans and activities

Fern
Unfaithfulness is possible in a lover

Fir tree
Success, especially in the arts. The higher the tree the better

Fire
Avoid over-hasty reactions, especially anger

Fish
One of the very best omens, this indicates good luck in everything

Flag
Danger threatens, particularly if the flag is black

Flower
A wish will be granted

Fly
Worry, especially domestic. The more flies there are the more varied the swarm of misfortunes

Forked line
Decisions must be taken. (Whether these will be successful or not depends upon the attendant symbols)

Frog
Avoid self-importance as it may cause trouble

Fruit
This is a lucky symbol, especially if the fruit is in season

Garland
Success and great honour

Glass
Integrity

Goat
Enemies threaten

Gun
near the handle — an attack will threaten domestic happiness
at the bottom of the cup — slander undermines the client
for military personnel — cancelled leave

Hammer
Ability to overcome obstacles and perhaps a tendency to ruthlessness

Hare
Over-timidity

Harp
Domestic harmony
for single people a harp indicates a love affair with a successful outcome

Hat
New possibilities, and probable success
if the hat is bent and holed — failure is more likely
if the hat is in the bottom of the cup — a rival

Hawk
Sudden danger threatens

Hill
Obstacle to progress. (Especially if clouds obscure it)

Horse
galloping — good news, especially from a lover
the head only — a lover

House
Secure conditions, especially in business, so a good time for new ventures
if the sign is near the handle and obscured — domestic strife or illness may threaten the family

Human figures
Consider these carefully and take your cue from their appearance, activities and the surrounding symbols

Insect
Minor worries, soon overcome

Jester
Avoid frivolity, it might be a disadvantage. A time for seriousness

Jug
Influence, enabling the client to give help to another
near the handle — excellent health

Kettle
near the handle domestic contentment
near or at the bottom of the cup — domestic strife

Key
Intelligent appraisal can see and seize new opportunities
double, or near the bottom of the cup — danger of robbery

Knife
Separation, broken contracts, ended friendships
near the handle — divorce
crossed knives — bitter argument

Ladder
Promotion, probably through hard work

Leaf
News
if the leaves are in clusters — happiness and good fortune

Letter
News
if obscured —bad news
if near dots — news concerning financial affairs

Light-house
Trouble threatens but will be averted before it strikes

Lines
Progress, especially if clear and straight

Lion
Influential friends and consequent success

Lock
Obstacle to your advancement

Man
near the handle — a visitor
with arms outstretched — bearing gifts

Mask
Take care, people are trying to deceive you

Mermaid
Take care, people are trying to tempt you

Monkey
Flatterers represent danger; they intend mischief

Monster
In any shape or form this indicates terror

Moon
full — a love affair
in first quarter — new projects
in last quarter — a decline in fortune
obscured — depression
surrounded by dots — marriage for money

Mountains
High ambition which will be successful if the peaks are very clear

Mushroom
Growth, expansion
near the handle — a new home in the country

Nail
Malice threatens and injustice may be inflicted

77

Necklace

complete — many supporters and admirers
broken — marriage or love affair may break up

Net

Beware of traps

Nurse

Illness threatens
if near the handle — dependants may fall sick

Owl

This evil omen indicates that new ventures will fail
at the bottom of the cup — disease and financial failure
near the handle — unfaithfulness destroys domestic harmony

Palm

Success, honour and respect

Parachute

Escape from danger

Parcel

This is represented by an oblong leaf and indicates a surprise. (The surrounding symbols will offer a clue as to the nature of the surprise)

Parrot

Scandal and gossip threaten

Peacock

with tail spread — possession of an estate
surrounded by dots — a life of luxurious ease
near ring — a rich marriage

Pear

Comfort and financial ease

Pentagon

Mental and intellectual balance

Pig

Mixed fortune. (Material success may bring spiritual or psychological disaster)

Pistol

Danger, perhaps moral danger, threatens

Pot

Service to society

Profile

Temporary friendship, or acquaintanceship

Pump

A generous nature

Purse

Profit, usually material
at the bottom of the cup — this indicates an unexpected loss

Question mark

Hesitancy

Rabbit

Timidity

Rake

Attempts should be made to tidy things up and regulate life-style and work methods

Rat

Treachery and loss, deceitful friends and resourceful enemies

Reptile

Treachery and malice threaten, especially from false friends

Ring

Self-sufficiency, completion, eternity
near the top of the cup — a marriage is indicated
near the middle — marriage is offered
at the bottom — a long engagement (but if a cross is nearby it is doomed to be broken)
two rings — plans come to fruition, projects work out

Saw

Outsiders will theaten domestic tranquillity

Scales

A lawsuit is likely
balanced scales — justice will be done
unbalanced scales — injustice will be suffered

Scissors

Separation, quarrelling
near the handle — domestic bickering

Ship
Good fortune and/or good tidings are on their way

Skeleton
Ill health, poverty

Snake
Hatred and enmity, vicious plots

Spade
Hard work, but success at the end of it

Spider
This indicates a determined, persistent character (but with some guile and cunning)

Square
Restriction, even imprisonment: either external, of the body; or internal, of the mind

Sun
Great happiness, success and power

Star
six-pointed — good fortune
eight-pointed — a bad omen, accidents and reverses may be suffered
five stars — success, but no joy
seven stars — grief

Swallow
Swiftness of decision
This also indicates unexpected journeys, leading to a happy outcome

Swan
Smooth and contented life

Table
Dinner, party, feast, social gathering
dots nearby — a conference on financial matters

Toad
Beware of flattery and flatterers

Tortoise
Over-sensitivity to criticism

Trees
Plans will be fruitful, ambitions fulfilled

Triangle
pointing upwards — success
pointing downwards — plans go awry

Trunk
A journey and fateful decisions

Umbrella
Shelter will be needed
if the umbrella is open it will be found, *if closed*, denied

Violin
Individualism, perhaps egoism

Volcano
Passions may erupt and cause harm

Vulture
Loss, perhaps through theft; danger, possibly from an enemy in authority

Whale
Pre-eminence and success, especially in business

Windmill
Success will be achieved through industry and hard work, not brilliance

Wings
News is expected. (The attendant symbols will suggest whether this will be good or bad)

Woman
Happiness and pleasure
more than one woman, scandal and gossip

Yoke
Domination threatens, so avoid being too submissive

Zebra
Adventures overseas. (An unsettled life is indicated)

Dice

These deceptively simple little cubes with numbers marked upon them have been held to be responsible for making and breaking men's fortunes. The random nature of Fate is believed to be nowhere more clearly expressed than in the throwing of dice. Every throw is apparently completely unpredictable. The Egyptians knew these ancient toys, so did the Greeks. And throughout Asia precious woods and metals were used to make them in order to add to their latent power.

Method of reading

Dice have been used for divination for thousands of years, and methods of reading them have passed through many variations. There are, however, two absolute rules. For divination there must be three numbered dice, and they must be thrown in complete silence. It is also generally believed that they run more freely when the weather is calm and the atmosphere cool.

The most common method is to draw a simple chalk circle on a table and then throw the dice on behalf of the person whose fortune you are telling. Dice that roll beyond the circle have nothing to say. Those that fall on the floor indicate that disturbed and vexing times are ahead, which will probably be darkened by quarrels. If all the dice roll out of the circle, they should be picked up and thrown again. However, should the second throw also yield no result, it might be as well to assume that Fate has nothing to communicate that day, and wait until a more propitious moment.

There are two general points to remember. If a number turns up more than once during a reading, it presages the arrival of significant news. And on the very rare occasions when one dice lands on top of another it is always a warning that extreme caution should be exercised in all commercial and romantic ventures.

Meaning of numbers

Once the three dice have been rolled, add together the numbers shown on them. If one has rolled outside the circle and the total is less than three, the dice have nothing to say. The list which follows gives the most familiar meanings of the total numbers.

Three A good omen.
A wish may be unexpectedly fulfilled.
Four Disappointment
Five A stranger will bring joy
Six Material loss from which some spiritual advantage may be gained
Seven Unfounded gossip will cause unhappiness
Eight A contemplated action has not been thought through, and may produce an injustice
Nine Success, particularly in amorous affairs. If there has been a quarrel, expect reunion, forgiveness, reconciliation
Ten Domestic contentment, and perhaps some professional or business advancement
Eleven Someone — not necessarily a member of the family or close friend — is ill
Twelve A letter will come, and an answer be demanded. Ask advice before coming to a decision
Thirteen Grief, probably protracted, perhaps even lifelong
Fourteen A stranger will become a close and dear friend
Fifteen Temptation to enter into a shady or unjust deal
Sixteen A journey. Take it, for it will pass pleasantly and end in profit
Seventeen A man from overseas, prob-ably a foreigner, will suggest a course of action to you. His suggestion will be sound
Eighteen A very good omen — promotion, profit and joy

Specific predictions

In order to make predictions more precise, you may divide the chalk circle into twelve parts. These twelve sections represent the following:
First section Next year's happenings
Second section Money matters
Third section Travel
Fourth section Domestic matters
Fifth section Present schemes
Sixth section Health
Seventh section Marriage
Eighth section Deaths — and legacies
Ninth section Present state of mind
Tenth section Work or profession
Eleventh section Friends
Twelfth section Enemies
Continue to take notice of the general message, read as above, offered by the three dice added together, and apply this to the particular sections in which the dice fall. They will probably fall in several sections, in which case the general message must be combined with those yielded by the separate sections. If two or three dice fall into one section this, of course strengthens the message they offer. The numbers on the individual dice are read as follows:
One Search whatever the dice say about this matter for indications of success
Two Success depends on friendly relations continuing
Three Success is bound to follow
Four Things will go badly, as far as this section's affairs are concerned
Five The indications are good
Six The problem under general discussion will in its outcome have a good effect on the matter covered by this particular section
There are no hard-and-fast rules about giving an overall prediction under this more specific method. The general message offered by the three dice must somehow be combined with the particular ones from the individual sections. Use your subtlety and intuition to bring this sometimes fragmented and almost incoherent information into an ordered and relevant meaning. It will be enjoyable to discover how much skill you have.

Dominoes

The pieces used in the game of dominoes can, like dice, reveal possible expressions of the operations of Fate. Here the diviner shuffles the pieces, face downwards, and draws one on behalf of the client. The piece is turned upwards and read according to the table below. It is then returned, face down, to the rest of the pieces, which again are shuffled. A second piece is then drawn and read. This operation may be repeated for a third time, but no more. If one draws more than three pieces at a consultation, or allows more than one consultation per person a day, the dominoes become tired and are liable to mislead you!

Meanings

Double Six Success in every way
Six/Five Charitable works
Six/Four Litigation which is unlikely to be successful
Six/Three Short voyage with a beneficial outcome
Six/Two A gift, likely to be useful and to be presented soon
Six/One An end to the root of all your troubles

Six/Blank Be careful — especially with those you think are your friends
Double Five A move to a new house or apartment, where happiness awaits
Five/Four Profits. But do not use these for speculative ventures
Five/Three A helpful visitor
Five/Two A child is born, probably within the subject's family
Five/One Love affair — passionate but ending unhappily
Five/Blank Give comfort to a friend in trouble
Double Four A party given by a stranger
Four/Three Expected disappointments need not be feared
Four/Two A swindler — perhaps a philanderer — has entered the client's life
Four/One Debts must be paid — even at risk of temporary poverty
Four/Blank Attempt reconcilliation with estranged friend
Double Three A rival in love. Distress and misery result.
Three/Two Avoid tempting fortune for a few days
Three/One Surprising news, of great usefulness
Three/Blank Jealousy makes trouble and disrupts friendship
Double Two Happy marriage
Two/One Loss of money or property, this to occur in the very near future

Two/Blank Meeting, a new relationship and consequent happiness
Double One Avoid hesitation; a bold decision awaits and should be taken
One/Blank A stranger, probably from overseas, who will be of use
Double Blank A bad omen — indication of loss, disappointment, unhappiness

Sometimes you will draw the same piece twice. This confirms the prediction and at the same time suggests it will happen very soon. Usually however, as so often with predictions, the dominoes offer fragments of information which you yourself must build into a coherent message.

Take as much care and time as you need in order to organize the diverse clues into a clear picture. Concentrate hard. Imagination and those latent psychic powers may very well help you to a surprising degree of accuracy.

Reading

The client is a middle-aged housewife, and Five/Four, Four/One and Six/Two are drawn in that order (see picture below), showing that she will receive a windfall. However, she will have to use it to meet old bills. To take away the sting of that, a present will arrive — which may or may not be all the better for being a useful one.

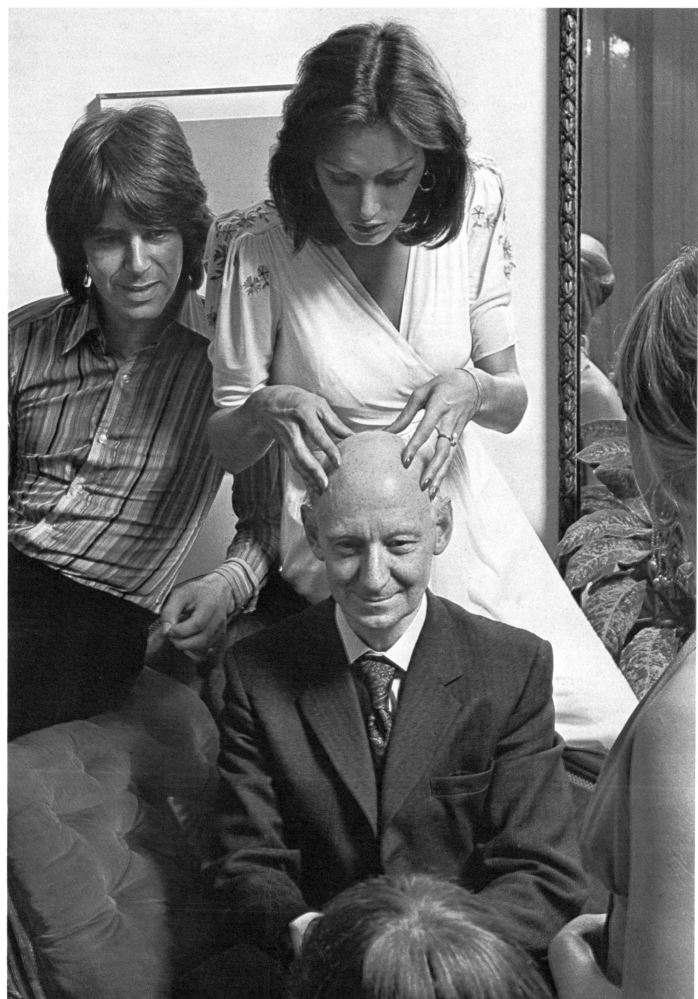

carrying them out—a steadiness perhaps not strong enough to restrain the impetuous.

Twenty-one Ambition achieved, freedom, independence; but in those whose Primary number is 3, it suggests overconfidence, impatience.

Twenty-two A strong number, increasing the significance of what the Primary number has indicated. It suggests dreams and false judgements, so it may lead to disaster.

Date of birth

In numerology, as in astrology, the subject's date of birth is important. This is to be expected as it is a personal set of numbers relating to the day on which he or she was born.

This date is simply converted to a Primary number. Just write the whole birth date out in figures, add them together once, then add together the result, until you are left with only a single figure. So, if the client was born on April 14th, 1945, the date in figures is 4.14.1945, which you write as the sum, $4+1+4+1+9+4+5$. The answer, 28 gives you the sum $2+8$, which in turn gives you the answer 10. And that, added together, gives the single number you need for the reading — the number 1.

Names

To give a deeper character analysis apply the divinatory power of numbers to the client's name and surname.

Numerical equivalents
This simple key gives a numerical equivalent for each letter.

A	B	C	D	E	F	G	H	I
J	K	L	M	N	O	P	Q	R
S	T	U	V	W	X	Y	Z	
1	2	3	4	5	6	7	8	9

Using this method the name 'Janet', for example, becomes 11552. Proceeding in the usual way this becomes the sum, $1+1+5+5+2=14$. These two figures added together give you the Primary number 5.

Numbers have always had ritual significance, especially in the religions that are based on the Bible. Left top: the Seven Angels bearing plague; bottom left: the Four Horsemen of the Apocalypse; bottom right: the Second Coming of Christ.

Follow exactly the same method to reduce a surname to a Primary number. However, when dealing with the second given name, omit the final stage because for this Secondary number you need a double figure.

When the second given name is too short or has too many A's to give a double figure, use 10 as an equivalent for 1, 11 for 2, 12 for 3, etc. Do the same when the name adds up to more than 22; that is, reduce it to a Primary, then find the double-figure equivalent. So, for example, if the name adds up to the figure 32, that would reduce to the single number 5, which gives you the Secondary number 14.

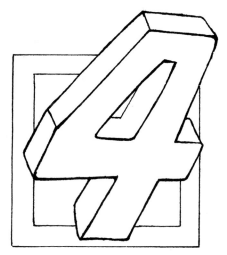

Cheiro's system

Cheiro, the famous French clairvoyant and palmist who lived and worked in the late nineteenth century, gives in his *Book of Numbers* a key which he claims may have originated with the Chaldeans. (Alphabets have changed so much since then that this is difficult to prove or disprove.) Here is his version.

A—1	G—3	N—5	T—4
B—2	H—5	O—7	U—6
C—3	I/J-1	P—8	V—6
D—4	K—2	Q—1	W—6
E—5	L—3	R—2	X—5
F—8	M—4	S—3	Y—1
		Z—7	

A full analysis

Once you have mastered the use of the keys and the meanings of the numbers you can give someone a full reading. To do this you reduce the client's birth-date, name and surname to Primary numbers. These, reduced again to a Primary number, give you the Character number — the key to the client's character. The client's second,

less-used, given name is reduced to a Secondary number and this tells you which character traits are strengthened or weakened.

Suppose, for example, that you have to analyze the character and prospects of a lady named Mary Pamela Waters, who tells you she was born on September 15, 1951. Following the procedure above her birthdate is reduced to the sum $9+1+5+1+9+5+1=31=4$.

Next ask her whether she is normally called Mary or Pamela. This will tell you which name gives you the Primary and which the Secondary influences. If it is 'Mary' which she most often uses, write that name and the name 'Waters' vertically, one below the other, then write beside the letters their equivalents in figures.

Using the first of the two keys above (not Cheiro's system), this would give you the following:

M=4
A=1
R=9
Y=7
Total: 21=2+1=
Primary number 3
W=5
A=1
T=2
E=5
R=9
S=1
Total: 23=2+3=
Primary number 5

Thus: total name number is $3+5=8$
birth date number is   4
—
Total=12
Thus: $1+2=$Character number 3

You now know that the main characteristics of Mary Waters are those associated with the number Three: conscientiousness, a strong sense of duty, an authoritarian streak. To find out to what extent these traits are modified turn to her less-used middle name. Using the same key this gives you:

P=7
A=1
M=4
E=5
L=3
A=1 Total: 21=Secondary number.

You discover that Mary's already strong personality is given even more force by her secondary characteristics: her individuality, her need for independence. In all, this analysis suggests that she will be a very successful woman, although her personal relationships might suffer.

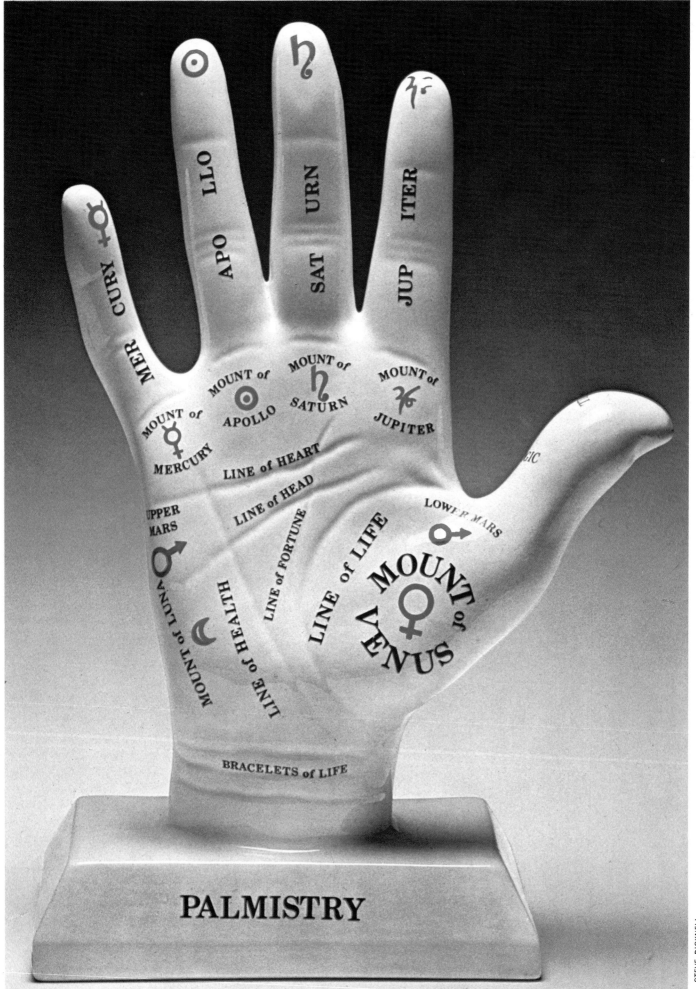

PALMISTRY

Palmistry: reading the hands

There are two aspects to palmistry. The first, called Chirognomy, attempts from the shape of the hand to analyze a person's psychological and emotional make-up. The second, Chiromancy, seeks to use the lines of the hand to foretell a person's future. Palmistry is very old. It was known in China over five thousand years ago, and some people think that it began there. Others believe that it was first practised either in Egypt or India.

Reading of hands is still widespread in modern India, and throughout the Middle East too. The Ancient Greeks knew of it — Aristotle certainly mentioned it, calling the hand 'the organ of organs'. It was known in Western Europe at an early stage, too. The first datable use of the word 'palmistry' was in a book written in English in the fifteenth century, but since books were rare at that time and seldom survived, it was probably used long before.

It is hard to be certain whether the lines of the palm actually foretell the future. That they, and the shape and structure of the hand, should give an indication of character is, however, much more plausible. From the literature on the subject, one can believe that some sort of connection has been more or less proved. Thus an analytical reading is likely to be more accurate, more useful and, in some ways, even more amusing than speculative prognostications of an uncertain future. Not only that: it cannot be repeated too often that such prognostications carry their own dangers. People tend to be credulous in these matters, nor need you believe that they are not when they protest their scepticism. Prophecies may, therefore, prove worrying for them and, in some cases, may alter their attitudes and plans.

Thus the palmist, however temporary and amateur, has responsibilities and should be aware of them and be very careful in the way they are discharged. A cautious silence is wiser than reckless forecasts of disturbing events.

Hand prints

A superficial reading of a hand can be done fairly quickly, but anything more detailed requires time. For this reason, and because it provides you with examples to study and learn from, it is a good plan to take prints of palms you want to examine. If you do this, anyone whose hand you decide to study does not have to sit still for the length of time that it takes to obtain a complete reading. This also has its uses when you want to read the hand of a child. The lines in the palms of children begin to be of significance during the first year — an age when they are not renowned for their willingness to keep still!

For a hand print you will need ink of the kind used in lino-cuts, a five-inch roller, a sheet of glass and a rubber pad not less than twelve inches square. Cover the roller in the ink, then roll it out on the glass to give it an even coating. Then ink the hand you want to examine. Try to cover it as evenly as possible. Have a sheet of good-quality heavy white paper ready on the rubber pad and press the hand to it, making sure that it does not slide sideways and so blur the impression. For the same reason, hold the paper firmly when the hand is raised from the paper. To start with, you may have to make several impressions before you have one good enough to use, but in a little while you will gain in confidence and skill.

There is another quick method, if you have access to certain types of flat copying machine. You can obtain a very good print in a few seconds, simply by laying your hand on the glass plate and operating the machine in the usual way. Care should be taken not to press the palm on the glass as this can obscure the lines. The samples given later in this chapter show how good the results can be.

For a time, most of the palms you examine will look strange and un-informative, but in time, like an explorer, you will learn how to fill in the blank parts of the map. For practice, you may be tempted to use your own palms, but in many ways this is unsatisfactory. We know ourselves — or we think we do. As a result, if we examine our own palms what we see must pass through that mesh of pre-conceptions, both flattering, and unflattering, that all of us have about ourselves. The habit of clear thought comes better from concentrating on the palms of other people. This is one reason why the ink and roller are so important.

Types of hand

Once you have the print — clear and yours to examine at leisure — what do you actually look for? First, apply the principles of chirognomy and consider the shape of the hand; the shape, length and placing of the fingers; and the position and prominence of the various mounds. This will enable you to assess the character of the subject. Take your time over this.

There are various ways of dividing the types of hand, but basically hands are either square or long.

Square hand

The square hand is one in which square fingers stem strongly from a square palm. This formation indicates practicality, a sense of order, a certain caution. People with square hands are generally practical, with their feet firmly on the ground. Their reliability will make them true friends and faithful lovers. Their liking for hard work, honesty and strength of purpose help them to do well in tasks that require physical effort. Their practicality and application are always indicated by the squareness of the palm, regardless of the length or shape of the fingers.

Long hand

The long hand, also called the conic or the artistic hand, usually has a slightly tapering palm, wider nearer the wrist, narrower at the base of the fingers. The fingers, too, taper gradually to rounded, cone-like tips. As a rule, such hands have small thumbs, and these indicate an impulsive temperament that can be inconstant. People with long hands tend to be very open to external influences and can become infatuated, with ideas and places as much as with people. Their moods can fluctuate between enthusiasm and dejection. Generous and sympathetic, they take up causes, sometimes of a revolutionary nature. They can be furious, but rarely for long, and they are not given to prolonged sulking. Because of the intensity of their feelings, they tend to pursue careers in the arts.

However, a hand that is too long and delicate can suggest that the depth of feelings may be greater than the staying power. For the artist, a better hand-shape might be tapering fingers rooted in a square and practical palm, or a long palm with square-ended fingers. Both these shapes promise a mixture of sensitivity and hard work which can lead to success.

Mixed characteristics

The subject of mixed hands is important in practical terms because not all hands conform to the theoretical purity of types.

Short fingers and long palm This combination suggests energy, speed of reaction, activity — especially if the palm is covered with many fine lines. But it also suggests impatience with the slower and less energetic. A person with this impatience may be somewhat at the mercy of his own versatility and there can be no doubt about his stability and reliability. People with hands of this type tend to choose individualistic, even unconventional occupations, certainly those which offer a variety of challenges and demand flair as much as application.

Long fingers and square palm The combination of long fingers and square palm is found in people who prefer reason to emotion, order to chaos. Such people put a possibly exaggerated emphasis on theory, on how things ought to be, without making enough allowance for how things actually are, influenced by human frailty, feelings and idiosyncracies. The work they choose, however, will usually be interesting and they will often show originality in it. They are, above all, the people to call on in problem situations. They may be teachers, journalists, even philosophers. Certainly they are often found in work that involves communication in one form or another.

Spatulate fingers Some hands, either long or short, have fingers shaped like spatulas, wider in the top segment than lower down. Sometimes their palms are of the same shape. This hand is usually a sign of great originality, combined with self-confidence and, often, creative energy, a mixture of qualities that is not suited to the solitude of a scholarly or artistic life. It is more likely to make people tend towards an outdoor life — an engineer, an explorer, or a successful soldier, for example, might have a palm and fingers of this shape. Some hands are truly mixed. Their fingers — short, long and spatulate — seem to have been brought together from various types of hand. When the mixture is marked, it points to a person of great versatility, someone who might also find it difficult to keep to one goal.

Other general features

Size of hand

There is also the size of the hand to be considered. Large hands suggest a reflective temperament, the ability to take stock before arriving at decisions. Small hands often belong to people who have a swift, intuitive awareness of the characters of those they meet, and of any decisions that must be taken, but who dislike finicky detail or laborious caution. They think big and act fast, and their haste can sometimes create problems for them.

Knotty joints

Knotty joints on the fingers suggest neatness, exactness, a power to observe and concentrate. They are said to be especially common on the hands of scientists.

Texture and elasticity

Make a note, too, of the texture of the skin of the hand you are studying. Fine skin can be a sign of sensitivity. When the skin of the hand is elastic and resistant it can be taken as an indication of energy and willpower. However, if the skin is very hard, this may suggest obstinacy and a lack of perception.

Flexibility

You may also take manual flexibility as an indication of mental flexibility, taking into account the age and occupation of the person whose hand you are studying.

The thumb

When you have come to a decision about the overall character of the hand, it is time to consider some of the details. First of these is the thumb, indicative of energy, symbol of the vital forces within us. A large thumb, therefore, suggests an energetic personality, making a forceful impact on the world.

The top, or nail, segment of the thumb, if it is particularly large, suggests a developed and powerful will and a great deal of staying-power. When this segment is rather narrow — and particularly if it is slightly pointed — the indication is of energies being uncontrolled and wasted.

The second segment, related to logic and reason, is sometimes markedly thinner than the top one, and this can indicate impulsiveness and a lack of control, a tendency to act hastily on impulse. Conversely, a thick, well-developed second segment suggests good control — even too high a degree

of it, great reasoning powers and consequent caution.

Consider, too, the relative lengths of the two thumb segments in order to see what balance there may be between energy and reason. When the thumb is set low in the hand, the energy it expresses is likely to be held back.

The fingers

Index finger

Since it is closest to the thumb, the index finger — or 'finger of Jupiter' — is often considered in conjunction with it. Also called 'the finger of ambition', it indicates the kind of desires for which the energy indicated by the thumb will be available and their strength.

A long index finger This suggests the desire to dominate and ambitiousness. If the energy of the thumb supports the ambition, the latter can result in a successful life, although not necessarily in a happy or well-adjusted one. If the energy indicated by the thumb is weak, however, then desire is likely to outreach grasp and this will result in feelings of failure and inadequacy.

Short index finger This, too, suggests feelings of inadequacy. When the finger belongs to a hand indicating a high degree of sensitivity, you can assume that you are studying someone retiring, meek and possibly put upon by others.

Straight index finger If the finger is straight this is a sign of well developed powers of observation, which will not be present if the finger is bent.

Curved index finger An index finger which bends towards the middle finger is a sign of a tendency to hoard and hold on to money. It shows a general lack of openness towards the outside world.

Middle finger

The middle finger, considered to be under the influence of Saturn, is a good indication of overall psychological balance. A long middle finger can be a sign of an over-intellectual approach to life. Conversely, a short middle finger indicates impulsiveness, a tendency to act on inner promptings rather than on a cool consideration of reality. The heavier and more dominating the finger, the more clearly it indicates seriousness and thoughtfulness. If the middle section is markedly larger than the other two, this indicates a love of the

Right: an intriguing and romantic party game — reading the palm of your favourite man.

country and of gardening.

Ring finger
This, the 'finger of Apollo', relates to the emotions and the better its shape and over-all balance, the steadier the psychological balance of the subject is likely to be. If the finger seems out of proportion with the rest of the hand, this may be a sign of an emotional life out of phase with the rest of the subject's existence. A very short finger, for example, can indicate difficulties in adjusting to other people, individualistic solutions to emotional problems, a nature given to arousing and even provoking conflict with others. A longer finger than expected points to a high degree of introversion and preoccupation with oneself and one's inner needs.

Little finger
The little finger, dedicated to Mercury, should be looked at in conjunction with the ring finger, the finger of Apollo, for it gives an indication of how well people are able to get on with others. Most important is its placing. If it is isolated from the other fingers, it indicates an inability to relate to other people and to form attachments. A long top segment to the little finger suggests fluency with words. If the finger as a whole appears a little twisted it can indicate untruthfulness.

Nails

The fingernails also have their significance. When they are short and broad with square tips, they indicate a high level of irritability and some degree of obstinacy. Short nails which are slightly rounded, however, suggest energy and a developed, even intrusive, curiosity. The long, oval nails of the dandy or the languid beauty indicate, as one might expect, no great energy, but a certain tolerance and an easygoing nature. They also show a high level of idealism and people interested in mysticism may well have nails of this kind. The larger the moons, the healthier the heart is likely to be. When the rest of the nail is very red in colour, the subject is likely to have a quick fierce temper. Better red nails than very pale, white ones perhaps, for the latter are thought to denote selfishness.

Palm contours : the mounts

Now look at the palm of the hand and the pads of flesh which give it its variations in contour. These are called the mounts.

The Mount of Venus
This lies between wrist and thumb and indicates energy. When it is fleshy and high, energy is strong and needs to be expressed physically rather than through thought or feeling. People with this form of mount, therefore, are often at their best working with their hands and muscles, particularly if they have a square-palmed, square-fingered hand. Alternatively they will tend to be very active sexually, although whether with one partner or with many only the rest of the hand can indicate. A well-developed Mount of Venus also suggests a high level of artistic ability, particularly when it is crossed by lines running towards the thumb from the Life Line.

The Mount of the Moon
Opposite the Mount of Venus, directly below the end of the Head Line, this also indicates energy, the energy of the imagination, which can feed creativity, although it does not guarantee it. In fact, when this mount extends well down the wrist, it suggests a sensitivity so extreme that it may inhibit all artistic work. But on a square hand,

MALCOLM SCOULAR

a well developed Mount of the Moon indicates imagination controlled by practicality, consequently it can indicate success in such careers as architecture or journalism. However, study of the rest of the hand may show that the imagination is uncontrolled and expressed in day-dreaming rather than definite action. The qualities of the Moon belong to the subconscious part of the mind and are passive ones.

The finger mounts

The mounts at the bases of the fingers are also significant in a full analysis of the hand.

The Mount of Jupiter
Situated below the index finger, this indicates ambition and a healthy self-confidence. When it is over-developed, however, it is a sign of arrogance and an excessive desire for prestige. If it is practically flat, it shows an almost total lack of drive and even of self-respect.

The Mount of Saturn
Rising below the middle finger, this is often difficult to see. When it is apparent, though, it indicates a serious temperament. If it is rather large, it can be a sign of a mistrustful, pessimistic outlook.

The Mount of Apollo
Lying below the ring finger, this mount suggests an even and cheerful temperament, as well as some artistic ability. If the mount is very high, then these characteristics may blur into one another and become excessive, taking the form of self-indulgence, affectation and greed, especially for attention. A flat mount, however, indicates a rather dull personality, insensitive to beauty and unmoved by anything that is subtle or that needs perception.

The Mount of Mercury
In its normal form this emphasizes the characteristics which are also indicated by the little finger above it — fluency, swiftness in the use of words, wit. When it is too high, it hints at a tendency to lie and to use trickery; when it is too flat, it points to a dull personality — without humour or quickness of thought, too ready to believe and easily tricked.

Mounts of Mars
Finally, there are the Mounts of Mars. The Upper Mount of Mars, between the Mount of Mercury and the Mount of the Moon, gives an indication of moral courage, although when it is over-developed, it can be a sign of bad temper and a tendency to inflict mental cruelty. Someone whose Upper Mount of Mars is flat is unlikely to stand up for any cause — not even his own.

The Lower Mount of Mars, lying between the Mount of Jupiter and the Mount of Venus, suggests self-control and calmness in difficult situations, the sort of cool courage which test pilots or rock-climbers often need. Too big a Lower Mount of Mars may belong to a bully, whereas too flat a mount may be a sign of cowardice.

Mount markings

Often the mounts of the palm and fingers have various shapes on them — crosses, squares, triangles and so on, formed by the fine lines which cover the hand. Of these, the square in particular is thought to be fortunate and to offer protection, while the criss-cross of a grille is thought on the whole to be unfortunate. A triangle is usually taken as a sign that a person has fortune on his side, but when the mount is marked with the cross and the star, the significance of this may depend on where exactly on the mount the marking is located.

Below: the positions of the main lines and mounts. Right: the meanings of the Mount markings.

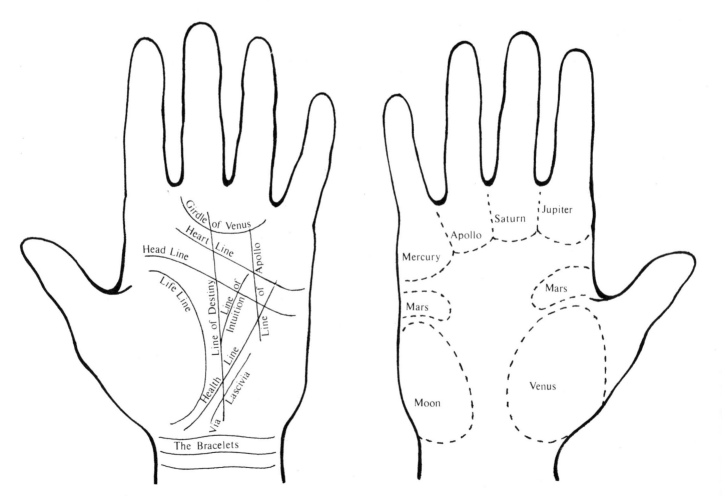

Some of the meanings of these marks are given in the chart below.

The main lines

Having studied the outline and contours of the hand, you will know something about your client, and you can now go on to read the lines of the hand. The three main lines are those of Life, the Head and the Heart. The information they supply will to some extent be modified and added to by the many other lines which cover the palm.

Right versus left hand

In a right-handed person the lines of the left hand indicate the qualities he or she was born with, and those of the right hand the qualities developed and modified by the efforts and accidents of life. In a left-handed person this is, of course, reversed.

Line of life

The Life Line runs from below the Mount of Jupiter and above the Lower Mount of Mars, starting from or bisecting the Head Line, and ending at the heel of the hand, pointing approximately to the middle of the wrist. As its name implies, it gives an indication of physical energy, vitality and strength, but it does not foretell the length of life or the time and nature of death. Nothing read in a palm is certain, partly because the lines themselves alter in varying degrees as time passes.

Life span Because a deep, sharply cut Life Line suggests health, energy and drive, this does indicate the likelihood of a considerable life span. A shorter line is not, in itself, the sign of a short life. It may merely mean a shortage of energy and a need to conserve strength. A line which moves in fits and starts, without being quite broken and with the sections interwoven, indicates variations in levels of energy. A person with such a Life Line will alternate between bursts of energy and periods of fatigue. If the line is really broken, there is a strong possibility that a severe illness or accident has happened at some point.

Ambition Where the Life Line begins has significance, too. If it begins higher than usual, actually on the Mount of Jupiter, it may be a sign of great ambition. Thinner lines cutting the Head Line and reaching up into the Mount of Jupiter also suggest ambition, although ambition probably backed by a sense of proportion.

Calculation If the Life Line begins by forking from the Head Line, the indication is that the energy will be controlled by calculation. The further along the Head Line that this fork occurs, the more control will be exerted. In extreme cases it reaches the point of cunning and results in a complete dependence on calculation, at the life expense of normal feeling and spontaneity. When the line begins below the Head Line, this can be taken as a sign of an impulsiveness that can seem almost uncontrolled at times.

Self-control A chain of lines between Head and Life Lines, before the Life Line breaks away to curve down on its own, suggests a tendency to inward questioning and too much self-control, mixed with periods of excitable, outgoing behaviour.

Line of the head

The Head Line starts halfway between the thumb and index finger, usually right at the edge of the palm, and either runs straight across the palm, stopping anywhere from halfway across to the other edge of the hand, or else curves downward to the Mount of the Moon.

Intelligence There could be some

	Square	Triangle	Star	Grille	Cross
VENUS	Love life without worry	Calculating in love affairs	*Mid-Mount:* sex-appeal; *near wrist:* difficult love life; *near thumb:* long devotion		*One, clearly marked:* a single lifetime love; *many:* a varied love life
MOON	Travel risk-free	Success, fame	Travel risk	Depression and tension	Travel risk
JUPITER	Success	Organizational skill	Unexpected success	Domineering character	Advantageous marriage
SATURN	No money worries	Problem solver	Tragedy threatens	Introspective, undirected	
SUN (APOLLO)	Good name safe	Fame, calmly taken	Influential connections	Vanity, attention-seeker	Disappointment, loss
MERCURY	No tensions	Can influence others, friendly	Success, especially for the studious	Cunning, even dishonest	Beware the dishonesty of others
UPPER MARS	No physical harm			Danger	Danger
LOWER MARS	Danger will not harm	Success in physical combat		Danger	Danger

link between the length and depth of the line and intelligence. It does seem to reflect the type of mind and the way in which this works. A long Head Line may be an indication of a broad and lively understanding. A short Head Line can be a sign of limited intellectual ability, but within the limits there may be intense activity and consequent achievement.

Concentration The depth of the line is what counts here. The deeper and more sharply cut it is, the greater the powers of concentration which it reveals. When the line is chained, this suggests bursts of concentrated mental activity. When it is doubled, with two lines running parallel, it can be a sign of a mind that is disorganized, perhaps to the point of being unbalanced.

Sensitivity A long, straight Head Line suggests a good memory and mental determination. When it slopes down to the Mount of the Moon, it reveals a sensitive temperament, probably in-

volved in the arts and certainly creative, but if it continues into the lower part of the Mount, it can be a sign of over-sensitivity, of an inward-looking nature that may suffer from depression.

Caution If the Head Line, as it begins, touches the Life Line, this is an indication of moderation and caution. The longer the two lines remain together, the more pronounced the caution is likely to be, so that decisions will be arrived at slowly and with difficulty.

Irritability If the Head Line crosses the Life Line, having begun on the Lower Mount of Mars, it reveals a tendency to irritability, although a Head Line straight across the hand is a sign that this tendency is at least partly controlled.

Independence Independence and brilliance of mind will show themselves in a slight gap between Head Line and Life Line, but if the Head Line then curves away to the Mount of the Moon,

these qualities may be limited by a changeable, over-sensitive temperament. When the space between the two lines is especially wide, there is reason to take this as a sign of recklessness, of a tendency to take independence and courage to the point of foolhardiness.

Self-expression A fork at the end of the Head Line suggests skill in self-expression, particularly through the use of words, and the more the line slopes towards the Mount of the Moon, the more marked that skill becomes. A line curving in this way, with a clear fork at the end, indicates literary ability. A three-pronged fork suggests diverse abilities — intelligence, creativity and also good commercial sense. Too large a fork, however, points to too much versatility.

Right versus left hand Check, too, the variation between the line shown on the left hand and that on the right hand. If there is a marked difference,

Thom Henvey   Age: 25   Occupation: Writer

Thom has an abundance of energy and strength. The fingers and thumb being fine show a fastidious nature in contrast with his obviously well-developed physique. Only things of quality will interest him for he has a critical eye, but he will be less involved with the material side of life as he gets older and his curiosity about the inner side of things.

His is rather a restless, vacillating nature which does not allow him to sit still for long. He has a lot of ideas, plans and projects which his well developed right hand, giving him energy — shown by the thick base of the hand and heavy finger of Venus — enables him to carry out.

Just about now, an extra Fate line is shown in his hands

indicating new responsibilities which he is about to take on himself, but the sound structure of the hands shows that he will cope successfully. It is possible that he is thinking of this new venture right now.

His Head Line is straight, clean cut, long and detached from the Life Line. This indicates success for it shows self-control, speed of thought, attention to detail and a very practical precise execution of work. He is capable of sustained mental effort and can burn the midnight oil with impunity.

His Line of Destiny indicates that at 29 success should be his. After that date Thom can afford to build on the foundation which he has already achieved.

this will show how much basic characteristics have been modified, and even distorted for the sake of making a way in the world.

Line of the heart

The Heart Line rises below the Mount of Mercury and runs across the hand, ending somewhere under or near the Mount of Jupiter. As its name implies, it gives some indication of the depth of feeling of which a person is capable. Its strength, length and depth relate to the profundity and steadiness of the emotions, and its position is important, too. The lower it is on the palm and the more curved the line itself, the more sexuality and sex-appeal will be apparent and the more zest and enjoyment will be shown in love-making. The curve of the line is important, however. If the Heart Line does not rise at the end but finishes a long way below the Mount of Jupiter, this is a sign of reserve and inhibition — an inability to be spontaneous and out-going. If the line ends by pointing upwards between the fingers of Jupiter and Saturn (the index and middle fingers), take this as showing a great enjoyment of physical pleasure.

Male versus female hands In a male hand, some feminity is indicated by a marked curve downward below the Mount of Jupiter. In a female hand, a similar curve suggests strong masculine elements.

Emotional balance If the line forks on and around the Mount of Jupiter, this has importance, too. A small fork on the Mount of Jupiter points to a steady emotional balance, and to the likelihood of a lasting, harmonious marriage. A wider fork, however, jabbing at the Mount of Saturn as well as the Mount of Jupiter, indicates changeability and self-absorption — a lack of interest in other people. Breaks in the Heart Line may show that there has been an illness of the heart at one time, or an emotional crisis, which probably ended inconclusively or unhappily.

Romantic predictions

Of course, it is in this connection that people most want to hear prophecies, so here are a few signs to look out for. Little lines branching from the Heart Line indicate romances and affairs — those running upwards being the happy ones, those dropping down from the line the ones which may prove miserable. A chained Heart Line shows at least one affair after marriage.

A break under the finger of Saturn means that a lover has left or will leave. A break under the finger of Apollo shows that it is the person whose hand you are studying who ends the affair.

Overlapping lines point to a quarrel and a break-up, but only a temporary one. A line running from the Heart Line and cutting through the Fate Line points to a marriage which will end unhappily. An island on the line under

John Fletcher   Age: 29   Occupation: Sales Manager

A great deal of duality exists in his make-up; the conflict is between wanting to go it alone and needing others.

His thumb indicates a very abstract way of looking at life. He likes to ponder things out a good deal. As a youngster, at home, he looked forward to the time when he would be independent. Now he is independent but the finger of Apollo clinging to that of Saturn shows a need for security and a great attachment to the family.

His constitution is not too good and he probably tires easily, but can overcome this by will-power rather than energy potential. This is also borne out by the innate love of fine detail shown in his hand — long Head Line on the left hand — which is his natural ability; and the desire to delegate such detail — short Head Line on the right hand.

He is very much an individualist and a rebel in his way of expression. His short Head and Heart Lines show he is undemonstrative. He expects to be understood by his actions rather than by his words. This being so, he tends to be misunderstood, but having a good measure of sensitivity (he has fine lines on his hands), he feels this acutely. Consequently his marriage could suffer. Success for John is a matter of harmonizing the dual sides of his nature — shown in the very different appearance of his two hands — and the sharp divergence between his private and public life.

the finger of Saturn suggests an unsatisfactory love affair, one that will bring little happiness. And an island anywhere on the Heart Line points to trouble in love affairs, emotional problems, sexual turmoil, but also to an underlying emotional stability.

Sexual relations The lines which mark sexual relationships run down the edge of the hand, at the side of the Mount of Mercury and between the middle finger. The fainter lines there indicate love affairs, the stronger ones marriages. When they run close to the Heart Line, they show that the affair or the marriage will happen early in life, probably before the age of thirty.

Emotional control Also important is the relation between the Head Line and the Heart Line, for sometimes the temperamental factors that govern these two lines may be in conflict. If the lines lie close together, the emotions are under the control of the mind. If the Heart Line lies very high on the palm, however, this suggests that emotion tends to overrule intelligence and that the subject has a possessive, even a jealous disposition. If a line connects the Head and Heart Lines, it indicates a violent and possibly destructive infatuation. Equally, a line which stretches from the Line of Destiny, the Fate Line, towards the Heart Line without quite reaching it suggests a love affair which will never end in marriage.

Marriage lines The lines indicating marriage also have their own important variations. A break in a marriage line has an obvious meaning, but if the ends overlap, the couple will come together again. If a marriage line curves towards the Heart Line, it is probably that the person whose hand you are looking at will live longer than whoever they marry. If there are tiny downward lines at right angles to a marriage line, your client's marriage-partner may have a long illness. An island on the marriage lines points to infidelity.

Children

Children are indicated by any firm lines which run down to the marriage line from the base of the finger of Mercury — the little finger — and the stronger any of those lines are the greater the likelihood that the child will be a boy.

Girdle of Venus

Sometimes a loosely chained, semi-circular line appears, looping from between the index and middle fingers to between the third and little fingers.

This is known as the Girdle of Venus, for it indicates a deeply passionate nature. The passion need not necessarily show itself sexually, for those with high ideals and an intense involvement in public causes may well have the Girdle on their palms. But it is usually taken as a sign of sexuality. As a result, in the nineteenth century when there was uneasiness about the sexual elements in human make-up, people thought the Girdle of Venus an indication of criminal tendencies and profound instability. Today it can be taken to be no more than a sign of sexual vigour, especially if it is supported by the evidence of a high Mount of Venus. A Girdle broken in the middle shows possible inconstancy, though this would have to be confirmed by other signs in the hand.

Line of Destiny

This line is strongly indicative of the kind of life which a person will live. In terms of character, a well-defined line suggests inner harmony, but a segmented and almost aimless line will be a sign of feelings of inadequacy and an inability to adapt to reality. The place to find the Line of Destiny is near the middle of the hand, running vertically from the wrist towards the middle finger. After adulthood, it changes little, particularly in anyone whose way of life is settled. As a result, the line is much used by palmists making forecasts about their clients' future.

Where it starts Discover where the Line of Destiny starts. If its starting point is almost off the palm, at the first of the lines which run round the wrist, it may belong to someone who has had heavy duties early in life. If it rises from the Life Line, this can be a sign of a cramping early environment, although, if the line continues strongly, this indicates success of life once independence has been achieved. A strong Line of Destiny rising from the Head Line can mean success rather late in life. When it starts from the Mount of Venus, this can show support from a loving family. When the Mount of the Moon is the starting-point, it can mean that help will come from outside the family — and that life will be made exciting but rootless by variety.

Where it ends See how the Line of Destiny ends. If it curves from the Mount of Saturn towards the Mount of Jupiter, you may be looking at the hand of someone who will achieve authority and power over others. If it curves towards the Mount of Apollo, it suggests fame and fortune to come. Any subsidiary line running upward

from the Line of Destiny may be taken as a good sign. Lines that run downward, however, show a likelihood of loss and failure. A Line of Destiny ending at the Head Line suggests eventual failure in life, largely through personal shortcomings and lack of forethought, while one ending at the Heart Line suggests unhappiness in love.

Crosses and linked, chain-like formations If these occur in the Line of Destiny they point to periods of difficulty: a cross at the beginning, for example, suggests a hard childhood, whereas a cross at the end can be a sign that old age will bring difficulties. Breaks in the line are a sign of personal upheavals, but when the fragments overlap, you can assume that the changes which they signify are chosen and not accidental ones.

Line of Apollo

Otherwise known as the Line of the Sun, this runs up from the wrist to the Mount of Apollo. It indicates by its strength good fortune and success. It does not give any clue as to which particular endeavours will bring luck but only indicates that whatever is attempted, good or bad, will have a successful outcome. It overrides by its mere presence many of the negative indications which may exist elsewhere in the palm. If you are reading the hand of someone tempted to become a gambler, a good Line of Apollo might make a sound basis for an otherwise chancy career.

The line should be clear and straight and unflawed. If it is broken or chained, its indications are reversed, for no venture is likely to last long enough to reach success. Naturally, there are few lines which are not flawed in some way, just as there are few lines which are totally successful. If it starts either on the Life Line or the Fate Line, the Line of the Sun indicates high honour and great wealth. When it begins on the Mount of the Moon, however, it tells that this success will be based on approval, amounting to worship, from the opposite sex. Pop stars and film stars are likely to have such a line. If the line rises from the Line of the Head, success will be later in life and will probably be based on intelligence, so the client could be a writer.

Markings on the line A star anywhere along the line of the Sun adds to the amount of luck which the line itself indicates. A series of bars near the beginning of the line shows that early life was hard. When they come later, they indicate the efforts of rivals to discredit your client. A cross, here as elsewhere, is a bad omen and shows that, for a while at least, luck can run out even for the most fortunate people. If the line breaks, look to see how strongly it continues after the break. This indicates no more than a temporary setback if the line is still clearly marked. But there is one sign which overshadows the good fortune shown by the line of Apollo — a deeply hollow palm. A very concave palm always indicates a continuing run of bad luck.

Line of intuition
The line indicating intuitiveness starts just below the little finger. It ends, having traced a shallow, semi-circular course, near the edge of the palm on the Mount of the Moon. If clear, it may be taken to show well-developed psychic powers, and a strong interest in the mystical and the supernatural. See

if the lines on the two palms differ. Someone who has the line deeply engraved on the right hand has worked at these intuitive gifts and developed them consciously. If the lines appear only, or in a much more developed form, on the left hand, intuition is rarely consciously resorted to, but operates subconsciously, prompting decisions which may later be rationalized.

Bracelets
These are the three lines running across the wrist that, if they are clear and distinct, indicate good health and a fortunate and peaceful future. If faint, they signify the opposite of this and if the one nearest the hand is chained, this suggests that a life full of struggle will be crowned by success. Marks in that top bracelet have their significance, too. A star there tells you

that a legacy may be expected. An angle, like a tick beside a correct sum, means something similar — money and honour — but not until after middle age, while a cross indicates a happy old age after a lifetime's struggle. The lines which begin in the top bracelet are also important. The one leading to the Mount of Apollo indicates a journey to the tropics, while that to the Mount of Mercury predicts unexpected wealth. Look for lines reaching up to the Mount of the Moon, for every one of them indicates that a journey will be taken.

Minor lines
There are a number of other lines, which are by no means invariably present in the palm. This does not matter, since their meaning will not affect a general interpretation.

Nicky Hayden   Age: 28   Occupation: Housewife
An impulsive, down to earth, and uncomplicated make-up is shown in the short, straight-set fingers and square palm.
Although she is very independent, she is also warm and instinctive. She could have married early, say at eighteen or nineteen years of age. And her strong Heart Line, taken together with the lines for children, seem to indicate a happy, meaningful relationship with probably three children — two boys and a girl.
She has a strong analytical ability — shown in her long finger

of Mercury — and should be good at working with figures as this would use her selective capacities to the full. She can discriminate and sort out what is relevant to the work on hand.
She can expect a change for the better at 28 as her Line of Destiny turns then to the left, and this will make her career more satisfying. And as she gets older she appears to develop the intuitive powers shown in her hand by the strong Line of Intuition.

Fortune in the cards

All playing cards are mysterious. Their curly-bearded kings stare up at us enigmatically, cryptic smiles on their faces. The familiar spades, diamonds, hearts and clubs are potent symbols with many hidden meanings. But what was their beginning? One tradition has it that they were invented by a concubine of the Chinese Emperor S'eun-Ho in 1120 AD. Another indicates that cards may have been used for divination in China two centuries earlier, having possibly come to China from India, crossing the Himalayas to enrich Chinese culture as Buddhism and Yoga had also done. In ancient India, cards were certainly used for augury, the packs being divided into ten suits — one for each incarnation of the Hindu god, Vishnu.

From the start, however, cards seem to have been used as oracles to help resolve people's personal problems. This function almost certainly preceded their association with play and gambling. Most of the skills of early civilizations had a religious aspect, and divination, as the word implies, involves the intervention of the gods.

Some of the European names for cards have derived from Middle Eastern words connected with prediction. The Hebrew word *naibi*, meaning sorcery, and the Arabic *nabi*, meaning to foretell, have given their name to an old Italian card game *naïb*, from which comes the Spanish word for cards, *naipes*. Indeed the Middle East provides another contender to the claim of having invented cards — the ancient Egyptian magician, Hermes Trismegistus. Whether he actually existed, or whether the stories surrounding him are mythical, is not certain, but there remains the possibility that it was under the Pharaohs of the Nile that cards were first employed in the endeavour to throw a little light on human destiny. This theory seemed to make sense when it was believed that the Gypsies originated in Ancient Egypt, for it was certainly the gypsies who spread the use of cards across Europe. But it is now known that the Gypsies first came from India, and so perhaps they brought cards with them from there, over two thousand years ago. Whatever may be the truth of their earliest origins, by the late Middle Ages cards were widespread throughout Europe. And there was a ready audience eagerly seeking their hidden messages—and has been ever since.

The pack

It was probably for the sake of convenience that the seventy-eight cards of the full pack were in the course of time reduced to the familiar fifty-two which we use today. For the art of foretelling the future by cards, known as cartomancy, it is usual to reduce the number to thirty-two. From the full pack, therefore, take the thirty-two cards which have a value of seven or higher, the ace counting as high.

What the individual cards mean

Each card has a meaning, and if you are going to be convincing it will be as well to familiarize yourself thoroughly with these.

It is necessary to remember, however, that certain combinations of cards have a meaning of their own, some of which are given later on. And any card may have its meaning altered by those which lie alongside it.

Since for centuries cartomancy has been mainly an oral tradition, there is bound to be a certain lack of precision, and there is some confusion about the exact meaning of a few of the cards. The most generally agreed meanings of what each of them stands for are given below.

Hearts
Ace Love, warmth, romantic and/or domestic happiness. Good news.
King A generous, handsome man, fair-complexioned.
Queen King's female counterpart, golden-haired and loving.
Jack Friend or lover — but perhaps not always to be trusted.
Ten Success. Good fortune — perhaps unexpected. Happiness.
Nine Fulfilment of hopes. A happy outcome.
Eight Invitation. Perhaps a journey or a visit. Often domestic contentment.
Seven Contentment, especially in marriage.

Spades
Ace Legal matters. A proposition in love or business.
King Lawyer — perhaps a little shady.
Queen Widow or divorcee, subtle and cunning.
Jack A dark, devious, even treacherous, young man.
Ten Worry, begun by a letter. Perhaps a journey — or even imprisonment.
Nine Failure and misfortune.
Eight Sorrow, usually caused by the receipt of bad news.
Seven Quarrels, turbulence — and the receipt of boring advice.

Diamonds
Ace Important letter — and/or ring.
King A man of power and strength.
Queen A gossip. Good-looking, but spiteful.
Jack A messenger, or a man in uniform.
Ten A change, probably a journey.
Nine News, probably concerning money and associated with some new enterprise.
Eight A short, happy journey. (In summer, perhaps a picnic.)
Seven An unexpected gift, or alternatively, hurtful criticism.

Clubs
Ace Success, particularly financial.
King A dark man, friendly and helpful.
Queen Warm, dark woman, affectionate and helpful. Perhaps a widow.
Jack A dark young man, sincere in love.
Ten Sudden money, as in an unexpected legacy.
Nine Financially good marriage.
Eight A dark girl or woman, who brings joy and good fortune.
Seven A small child, perhaps associated with money.

Meaning of suits

Sometimes, when you are laying out the cards, one suit figures more prominently than the others. When this happens, that suit's predominant influence to some extent alters the significance of the other cards. This means that they must be read in the light of that influence. Consequently, it is necessary to know what general feeling is conveyed by each suit.

Hearts
Love, affection, friendship, family and marriage. The emotions, particularly

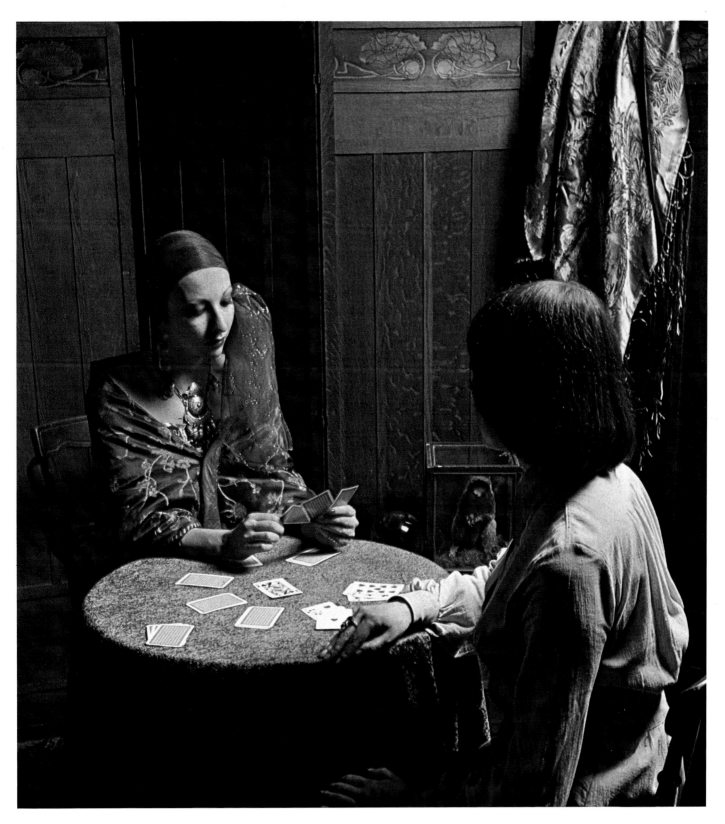

the warmer, more positive ones. Court cards correspond to people with blond or auburn hair.

Spades
Misfortune and warnings of misfortune. Enemies, scandal and betrayal, suffering and loss. Court cards correspond to people with dark hair.

Diamonds
World affairs, but rarely touching the

extremes of either circumstance or emotion. Court cards correspond to people with blond or auburn hair.

Clubs
Information mainly about friendship, loyalty and money. Thus also worry, anxiety and betrayal. Court cards correspond to brown-haired people.

Client card
The corespondence of court cards to

particular complexions and hair-colourings makes a basis for the selection of one card to represent the person whose fortune you are telling. This card is known as the 'client card'. A fair-haired young woman will be represented by the Queen of Hearts, a fair-haired young man by the King.

An elderly woman with fair, red or grey hair will be represented by the Queen of Diamonds, and a man of similar type by the King.

Dark-haired young men and women are represented respectively by the King and Queen of Clubs.

Dark-haired elderly men and women are represented by the King and Queen of Spades.

The meaning of the other cards can then be related to the way they lie in juxtaposition to the client card.

Here are some examples of the way this works. If your subject is a man and his client card lies next to the Queen of his own suit, this suggests that he will marry soon. If the Queen of Hearts lies next to it, his love will be true, deep and long-lasting. If the Queen of Spades, it suggests a furtive and perhaps guilty affair. If the Queen of Clubs, that he will form a relationship, perhaps a deep friendship, with a wealthy woman.

The Jack of Diamonds next to his client card points to a secret love affair; the Jack of Clubs to money troubles; the Jack of Hearts to some unfaithfulness, and the Jack of Spades to the threat of dishonesty by work colleagues, particularly subordinates. If your subject is a woman, marriage is indicated when her client card lies beside a King of the same colour. A King of the opposite colour suggests a secret love affair. The Jack of Hearts points to a flirtation. The Jack of Diamonds indicates a short-lived infatuation, and the Jack of Spades means an unhappy involvement with a predatory male. If Jacks keep appearing in her cards, the indications are that she may be somewhat indiscriminate in distributing her favours. Whether you mention this will depend on your sense of honesty.

Interconnected meanings

Certain other juxtapositions of cards have an especial significance. The Ten of Diamonds near the client card points to a journey. Near to the Ten of another suit, it suggests a legacy. Near to the Ace of Diamonds, it means a letter, probably from abroad. The Ace of Diamonds itself, when next to the Nine of Spades, indicates a threatened illness. And when next to the Seven of Diamonds, an impending quarrel of some violence. The Ace of Spades near both the Eight and Nine of Spades gives a gloomy reading, suggesting that the future will be heavy with disappointments — friends will betray, business will falter or even fail, deals and arrangements will threaten to collapse.

The Eight of Diamonds raises promises of travel — near any Heart the journey will be short, but near any Club it will be prolonged. If the Seven of Diamonds lies near any Club, the indications are that money will cause problems. A Nine of Diamonds near the client card suggests a path strewn with obstacles. While if the client card is near the Nine of Spades — traditionally a sinister card — there will be bad news and the possibility of illness.

Pairs, triplets, quartets

It is of particular significance when cards of the same value are laid down in pairs, threes, or — most powerfully — fours. These should be looked for first, since the message given by the cards as a whole will be influenced by their meanings.

These meanings have been subject to traditional variations, but the following are the ones most favoured:

Aces
Two Forthcoming marriage.
Three Minor love affair, or flirtation. According to some, excessive credulity.
Four Success.

Kings
Two The portents are good.
Three Considerable success, especially commercial.
Four Great success in all endeavours.

Queens
Two Friendship, but gossip threatens.
Three A visit, but there is jealousy and back-biting.
Four Menace of scandal and slander.

Jacks
Two Bickering will break out.
Three Disharmony, especially within the family.
According to some, laziness.
Four Vicious and upsetting quarrels.
According to some, success.

Tens
Two Receipt of an unexpected, but probably small, sum of money.
Three Financial and/or legal problems.
Four Good fortune, particularly perhaps in a career.

Nines
Two Limited success, particularly financial.
According to some, obstacles.
Three Success.
According to some, boredom.
Four A fortunate surprise.

Eights
Two Trouble and argument.

Three Family problems.
Four An anxious, frustrating time.

Sevens
Two An old enemy appears — or perhaps a new lover.
Three A baby will be born.
Four Enemies encircle.

Laying out the cards

Now that you have some idea of what to look for in the cards, what are the forms or shapes in which they should be laid out?

Over the years there have probably been hundreds of ways, as seers and experts frequently devise their own variations. But to start with it is best to use a few methods, each simple to follow, which provide clear readings. These readings must always be supplemented by your own intuition. In order to aid this elusive faculty, the readings must be done in an atmosphere of intense concentration, in itself an aid to belief.

It is always a good idea to ask your subject to shuffle the pack before cutting it because this directs his or her attention closely on to the cards and creates a feeling of expectancy.

Cutting the pack

Cutting is traditionally done with the left hand, because the mystic forces which add to the divinatory power of the cards are supposed to flow through the left, or sinister, hand. The subject should certainly always cut the cards, even if he or she does not shuffle them.

Reading your own cards

By and large, it is not advisable to use the following methods of laying out cards for trying to divine your own fortune. Traditionally they are intended to answer the questions of others, using powers and energies for which you are supposed to be the neutral channel.

There are, however, a number of games of patience (solitaire) whose object is to give answers to one's own questions. Usually these work on the basis that if they do not come out, the answer is 'No', and circumstances are not propitious.

The wizard
One method which seems to demand a fair amount of co-operation from Fate is known as the Wizard. You take the thirty-two card pack and begin laying down the cards face upward. As

you lay down the first card, you say out loud "Seven". Then as you lay down the next card you say "Eight", and so on until you have called "Ace", when you start again with "Seven". Whenever you actually lay down a card which corresponds to the value you have called, put it to one side. Keep going through the pack until it is exhausted — or until you are.

The more swiftly you and Fate discard the cards, the better augury it is. If the cards and your calling do not coincide at all, or only at very long intervals, you may assume that your project is, for the time being, unlikely to prove successful.

Reading other people's cards

Some of the methods of laying out cards for divination for a client follow. The one thing that they all have in common is that you need to use your imagination and intuition to interpret the messages they have to offer.

It is for this reason, as well as to foster confidence, that you should learn the meanings of the cards by heart. Only when you have them immediately available will you be able to string them together into coherent and evocative predictions.

Cartomancers have a saying that the cards get tired, and this may be true if they are really under some external influence. Many people believe in the existence of psychic powers, and cartomancy is one way to concentrate them if you have any. But it seems they should never be abused by too much use, or by a shallow approach.

Limit your card readings, therfore, to one session an evening, or at most two, divided by a period of rest. Only do some half-dozen readings at each session. If the other people present want to hear what you see in their cards, let them wait for a future occasion.

Finally, one small warning. People take predictions of this sort more seriously that they themselves may realize. If you find yourself faced with what seems a very gloomy forecast, reflect if a little diplomacy might not be in order. Illness or bankruptcy are serious subjects. And while warnings are not threats, predictions have a way of influencing behaviour, If, therefore, you are faced with a row of cards heavy with Spades, you might be well-advised to make a compromise between honesty and optimism. A little consideration for your friends' peace of mind cannot come amiss.

The fan

For this method, spread the cards face down on the table, and ask the subject to draw thirteen at random.

Take these thirteen cards and spread them face upward, in a fan shape.

Look to see if the client card which represents your subject is there, or the seven of the same suit which may act as its substitute. If neither appears, you can either begin again or take it as an indication that the moment is not propitious for divination.

Taking the client card first, count the cards off in fives, from left to right, reading every fifth card, and always using the card you have just read as the first of the next five. (Naturally you do not read the client card, but continue until you have read all the other twelve.) Next ask the inquirer to pick five more cards from what remains of the pack left face down on the table. Spread these out face upward in a separate fan. These cards are read in pairs. The first and fifth together, then the second and the third. The middle card is read by itself.

Reading

Here is a reading of the cards which appear in the photograph opposite, top. The inquirer is a fair-haired girl, so the client card will be the Queen of Hearts.

First consider the cards as a whole. Clubs predominate — although only slightly. Bear in mind that money may be important in the reading. There is a pair of Sevens, and these might indicate a new lover — or an old enemy — erupting into her life.

Beginning with the client card, and counting off the cards in sets of five, the first card to be read is the Seven of Diamonds, indicating a gift, and this is followed by the treacherous but darkly handsome Jack of Spades. Then the bait of an advantageous marriage is dangled by the Nine of Clubs. The Seven of Hearts indicates contentment in marriage — a trait not normally connected with the Jack of Spades.

The Seven of Clubs gives a child associated with money. This may be involved with a legacy, for it is followed by news about money indicated by the Nine of Diamonds.

From here on, the marriage signs become clearer, for in the Jack of Clubs a new suitor appears, honest and sincere. He is more the type to lead to the contented marriage already indicated and he may well be the lover indicated by the adjacent pair of Sevens.

The Nine of Hearts suggests that hopes will be fulfilled, a suggestion reinforced by the Eight of Hearts with its hint of domestic felicity.

The Ace of Clubs offers financial success, probably by way of the Ace of Spade's new proposition. This could possibly be made by the affectionate, although widowed, Queen of Clubs. (She could be understood to be the new lover's mother.)

All this is confirmed by the first pair of the supplementary five cards, the Ten of Clubs suggesting unexpected money, and the Ace of Diamonds an important letter.

But now there is bad news. The money may have to do with someone's illness, perhaps even the death of someone close because the Ten and the Eight of Spades in juxtaposition make a formidably unpleasant pair. But the King of Diamonds is a man of power, a tower of strength. If your subject trusts in his ability, she will come through this final crisis.

To summarize this information:

First, the client is being pressed to marry a young man whom she does not trust because it would be financially advantageous for both of them to do so. She should resist, for a new and truly loving suitor will appear through whom both happiness and money may be hers. Nevertheless, a crisis is brewing. Someone close to her is likely to be very ill, and an anxious time will follow. She should trust the strong man, friend or relation, who will appear at that time to help her bear the strain.

The seven cards

After your client has shuffled and cut the pack, draw out each seventh card, putting the six cards in between to the bottom of the pack each time.

When you have twelve cards, spread them out from left to right in the order in which you draw them.

Select the client card. If it is not there, take it from the remainder of the pack. If it is there, draw a thirteenth card at random from the pack and lay it with the others.

Beginning with the client card, count off seven cards, reading the last one. Continue in this way, reading every seventh card. When you have read all the cards, shuffle the thirteen cards again, and ask the client to cut them (with the left hand, of course). Spread the top six cards face upwards in a line. On the first five of these, place one additional card, leaving the sixth by itself. Then on the first two, lay down

two cards which you have left.

The first little stack of three cards represents the subject as a person. The second stack of three cards stands for the house or apartment he or she lives in. The next stack of two cards shows what is expected to happen. The fourth stack represents what is not expected, the fifth stands for the real surprises that are lying in wait. The final, single, card will tell your subject's thoughts or wishes.

Reading

Opposite (below) is the second stage, the 'seventh cards' having already been drawn. The client is a man, well-set-up, middle-aged (his client card was the King of Clubs), who is married.

Begin with the three cards on the left, which relate to him directly, and they tell us that he made a financially helpful marriage (Nine of Clubs) with a warm, affectionate lady as dark-haired as himself (Queen of Clubs) and that he either likes travel and change or has very recently come back from a significant voyage (Ten of Diamonds).

Next, his house: it is a source of worry, sometimes feels like a prison (Ten of Spades), he has a neighbour who makes him feel uneasy (Jack of Hearts), but his house has accommodation for a child, probably a nursery.

He nevertheless expects, the next column shows, to remain contented in his marriage (Seven of Hearts) and anticipates seeing someone close to him in uniform (Jack of Diamonds).

There are shocks in store, coming by way of an unreliable lawyer (King of Spades) — but the outcome will be unexpectedly happy (Six of Hearts).

A relationship, perhaps a marriage, between two mature friends of his, both with a great capacity for affection (King of Clubs and Queen of Hearts) will be the real surprise the next few weeks will bring.

Then, his wish. Here the Eight of Hearts echoes the Ten of Diamonds in the first column: what he really wants is the chance to travel.

The mystic star

From the thirty-two cards, pick out the client card and lay it face up in the middle of the table.

Your client, having shuffled the rest of the pack, cuts it twice, placing the resulting three piles face downward. You then turn each pile the right way up, and read the top cards thus revealed, first one by one, then in combination. This is called a general

indication and will give you an overall idea of the way fortune is running for your subject. The client now reshuffles the pack.

You take the top eight cards and, in an anti-clockwise direction, lay them face downward at regular intervals around the client card, which still remains in the centre of the table. It is in this way that you form the mystic, eight-pointed star.

Your client now takes the rest of the pack, and on each of the eight cards lays two more, working round the circle twice and setting the cards face down one at a time.

One by one, still working anti-clock-wise, turn each little stack of three face upward. Read the information all three cards provide in conjunction.

Reading

The client card, the Queen of Spades, shows that we are considering the fortune of a dark, middle-aged, married lady.

The general indication, which was gleaned from the Nine of Spades, was of changes, with some steep ups and downs likely.

The first column, directly above the client card, certainly suggests a down-turn in fortune: a shady lawyer (King of Spades) and a man of power (King

of Diamonds) combine to bring about the client's failure (Nine of Spades). Moving leftward, we discover news (Nine of Diamonds) of a romance (Ace of Hearts) involving a very dear friend, probably blonde (Queen of Hearts). Since she is known for her generosity, it is probably her gift (Seven of Diamonds) which leads to a journey (Ten of Diamonds), almost certainly to visit her and discuss the financially advisable marriage (Nine of Clubs) which is in the offing.

But what of the client's own life? A new proposition (Ace of Spades) leads to an unexpected success (Ten of Hearts), one of the sudden ups in her fortunes, which in turn gives her the chance of another journey (Eight of Hearts).

Can it be this which leads to domestic quarrels (Seven of Spades)? If so, financial success, already indicated above, now appears again (Ace of Clubs) and married happiness results for her (Seven of Hearts).

Yet now a new worry will appear, which seems to involve her daughter, the dark girl (Eight of Clubs). A letter arrives (Ten of Spades) concerning a dark young man (Jack of Clubs) who loves the girl. Correspondence ensues, for the Ace of Diamonds points to a very important letter — probably from the dark, friendly man (King of Clubs) who appears to be the young man's father. And the King of Hearts, a generous, affectionate friend, takes a hand in the affair. Despite the intervention of the spiteful and gossipy Queen of Diamonds, the arrival of the young man's mother, warm and likeable (Queen of Clubs), leads on to a short, happy and joyful journey (Eight of Diamonds) which one can only suppose will be taken to the sound of wedding bells.

To summarize, despite an initial setback in a legal matter, a new venture will lead to financial success and domestic contentment. A friend will seek advice about a proposed marriage, and the client's own daughter, after a short period of anxiety, will go happily to the altar with the approval of almost everyone concerned.

Single question

There are a number of systems for answering one question at a time. Let the client ask his or her question. There are then several methods of seeing how the cards will answer it.

Four Aces

One involves the four Aces. After your client has shuffled the thirty-two card pack, lay the top thirteen cards face up on the table, putting aside any Aces. Gather up all the cards again, having shuffled them as before, lay out another thirteen from the top, and again pick out any Aces. Repeat this a third time. Be careful to keep the Aces in the order in which they have appeared. The sooner the Aces do appear, the better for your client. The order in which they appear is very significant, the early cards having greater power than the later.

Thus the Ace of Spades, if picked out first, overshadows the other three, meaning nothing will be achieved without difficulty.

First seven cards

An even shorter method of answering a particular question consists of laying the first seven cards of the pack face down in a row, then turning up the first, fourth and seventh cards. These will provide the information you need for your answer. But here, of course, you need to remember the meanings of individual cards, as well as the significance of each suit.

Sometimes, of course, the answers given by the cards seem to make no sense at all. If this happens, you must remember that the information they are offering has to do with the future, in which there may well be other factors involved which will give the cards an unexpected relevance. So it is always a good idea to note down which cards have appeared, for they may yet become important.

However, if they do seem to be jumbled and meaningless, it is permissible to lay them down a second time, but no more. If on the second occasion too they reveal nothing, that must in itself be taken as a message. Like any other oracle, the cards reserve the right to keep their silence.

Reading

The commonest single question, of course, concerns love and its ramifications.

With the layout below a young lady asked the plainest question of all: 'Does he love me?' The Ace of Hearts, telling of warmth, domestic happiness and affection, seems to give the answer she is hoping for. But who is the dark lady, helpful and friendly, for which the Queen of Clubs must stand? 'Oh, his mother — she likes me', the girl says, at once. The Seven of Diamonds stands for an unexpected gift. In this context, almost certainly an indication that the young man will himself, quite suddenly and quite soon, indicate how he feels.

The weekly forecast

For this it is not necessary to learn the individual meanings of cards. All that is needed is an awareness of what the four suits as a whole represent.

Ask your subject to shuffle and then cut the pack into three piles. Take the top card of each pile, and lay it face down on the table in front of you. Begin with the left-hand pile, and end with the right.

Take the remaining cards in the three piles, ask the client to shuffle and cut as before, and once again place the top card from each pile face down on the table. These should be placed alongside the original three, so that there is now a row of six.

Repeat this operation three times more, so that you end up with a row of fifteen cards.

Turn over the two cards at either end of the row. These will give you the general fortune for the following day, determined by the symbols and colours revealed. The right-hand card relates to the morning, the left-hand card to later in the day. (If you had Spades on the right and Hearts on the left, it might suggest early disaster, followed by affection or comfort later on.)

Working inwards, two by two, gradually turn up fourteen cards. These will give the seven day sequence of the week's fortune. The points value of each card may be important, for if the suit is unlucky, as Spades tend to be, the numbers revealed should be avoided on the day in question. Equally, numbers in a lucky suit should be followed up.

This leaves the central, fifteenth card still face down on the table. Use it to answer a question — the suit of the card will give you the reply. If your subject is anxious about some action to be taken in a love affair, a Heart would be an encouraging card to turn up. While for someone with a business query a Club would be preferable. For all questions, a Spade suggests that postponement of any plans might be the safest course.

Reading

A forecast of this kind was done every Sunday for the manager of a small factory. In this instance the Diamonds show for the next two mornings that conditions for business during these first days of the week remain equable. The evenings, meanwhile, display Hearts, which suggests that affection, perhaps love, will flower then.

The third day, Wednesday, has Clubs all day: a worrying day with some money problems seems likely. The next morning, Clubs persist — perhaps there is also a question of loyalty to a friend and a colleague, probably a woman, which must be decided. By the afternoon, however, the King of Hearts indicates that their friendship is restored. Saturday morning is a good time, with Diamonds back on display, to catch up on work lost during the midweek crisis; the afternoon, however, produces more problems, perhaps at home or with a neighbour. This is, if anything, intensified on Sunday morning when there is scandal in the offing, double-dealing, possibly domestic strife. By the afternoon, however, things seem on an even keel once more, and the client can relax and prepare to start work the following week.

The central card remains, answer to a single important question. On this occasion the man asked whether he should employ a particular young man. Clubs indicate steadfastness and loyalty, so the answer here is affirmative: the man should be taken on.

Temple of fortune

This more elaborate method was invented by a famous cartomancer in pre-Revolution Paris, when the glories of the mid-eighteenth century were collapsing in the uncertainty which preceded the storming of the Bastille. Ask the client to shuffle and cut the pack as usual, then lay it out, each card face upward, in the following manner.

Starting at the bottom of the column, lay six cards sideways, one above the other, on the right-hand side of the table. Similarly, lay six cards sideways, one above the other and starting at the bottom, on the left-hand side of the table.

Now place four cards sideways, again starting from the bottom, immediately to the left of the first column, in such a way that these four cards are opposite the spaces between the lower five cards of the column.

Now place five cards in the upright position, from right to left, in a row which is level with the top card of the right-hand column, thus making a connecting row with the top card of the left-hand column.

Now lay down another four cards, sideways again and working from the top, immediately to the right of the left-hand column, so that they lie opposite the spaces between the lower five cards of the right-hand column.

Finally, above the connecting row of upright cards, lay another upright row consisting of the last seven cards of the pack.

The two rows of sideways cards on the right reveal the past. The two rows of sideways cards on the left reveal the future. And the two rows of upright cards are concerned with the present. The three outer rows of cards give the primary indications in each case. The inner rows modify what the outer rows tell you. The order of the cards is, as always, of some significance. They should be read in the order in which you laid them down.

Below: The arrangement of cards which gives the weekly forecast discussed in the text. Above right: A temple of fortune — one of the more elaborate ways of reading the cards which is described in detail here.

The mysterious Tarot pack

LE MAT.

LE BATELEUR

L'AMOUREUX.

LE CHARIOT

LA JUSTICE

L'ERMITE

TEMPERANCE

LE DIABLE.

LA MAISON DE DIEU

L'ÉTOILE

II

JUNON.

III

L'IMPERATRICE

IIII

L'EMPEREUR

V

JUPITER.

X

LA ROUE DE FORTUNE

XI

LA FORCE

XII

LE PENDU

XIII

LA MORT

XVIII

LA LUNE

XVIIII

LE SOLEIL

XX

LE JUGEMENT

XXI

LE MONDE

Most people regard Tarot cards with a degree of awe. Their age-old designs and symbols, their haunting figures, are deeply rooted in myths which remain mysteriously just beyond the boundaries of certain knowledge. It is easy to believe what these cards tell us and, involuntarily, to handle them with a feeling of solemnity, a sense of taking part in a very ancient ritual. Curious, and sometimes anxious, people have for many centuries consulted the Tarot. Partly because of their long history, and partly because of the power with which history has invested them, the Tarot cards are accepted by many people to whom no other system of fortune-telling makes the slightest appeal. It is, in a sense, the aristocrat of oracles.

Origins of Tarot

No one knows where these mysterious and potent cards were first devised. They have, however, consistently been linked with the Gypsies, who have long been regarded as the guardians of a secret branch of knowledge. This knowledge may have come from religious mysteries of pagan Greece, or the divine lore of the Chaldeans. What is true, is that both Tarot and Gypsies seem to have appeared in Europe during the period between the eleventh and fourteenth centuries.

Jacques Gringonneur, a fourteenth-century astrologer, sometimes credited with the invention of playing cards, almost certainly based the pack he devised for Charles VI of France on the Tarot.

The modern Tarot pack is based on the researches of an eighteenth-century French scholar named de Gebelin. His book *Le Monde Primitif* contained illustrations of the cards. It is this 'Marseilles pack' from which almost all the other Tarot packs used in the West have been derived.

The position of the Joker in the sequence has caused a certain amount of controversy. Many authorities have written works on the significance of the cards. But, untroubled by these discussions and differencies, Gypsies and others have used them to read the characters and fortunes of the thousands of people who have come to consult them.

Each pack of Tarot cards comes with instructions and interpretations. These are sometimes somewhat briefly or quaintly expressed, so below there is a simple explanation of the meanings of the cards.

Some people maintain that you should memorize all these meanings but you can, of course, refer back to the written word. And sceptics may be more inclined to believe your predictions if they see you referring to a text and interpreting it rather than apparently making the whole thing up as you go along! Belief depends a great deal on atmosphere.

The Major Arcana

The twenty-two cards of the Major Arcana, the Trumps, are subtle and complex symbols. They have a relation with the twenty-two letters of the Hebrew alphabet and the twenty-two branches of the Tree of Life which has a very prominent place in the Kabbala.

The Fool
Appearing anywhere, this card alters the meaning of the others. It is the free force in life, for it offers the inquirer a choice between good and evil, wisdom and folly.
Reversed: The choice may be bad and thoughtless.

1. Magician
Organization, control over natural forces, hence willpower. Suggests creative, perhaps artistic, ability.
Reversed: Weakness, force used destructively.

2. Priestess
The unseen, reached by divinatory power, thus an indication of unseen influences at work. Intuitive ability.
Reversed: Self-love, vanity, sensuality, superficiality.

3. Empress
The Earth Mother, thus fertility and marriage, wealth, the proper material rewards of endeavour.
Reversed: Barrenness, endeavour thwarted, resources dwindled.

4. Emperor
Determination, leadership, authority. The aid of powerful allies. A strong but well-controlled and directed sexuality.
Reversed: Immaturity, lack of control, subservience.

5. High Priest
Otherwise called the Hierophant or Pope. Stands for formal subjects: theology, ritual, law. Thus, acceptance of the conventions and hence social and material success.
Reversed: Inventiveness.

6. The Lovers
Harmony, balance between inner and outer, sacred and profane. Thus choice, based on attraction, hence success in love and — probably — marriage.
Reversed: Disharmony, unfaithfulness quarrels, perhaps divorce.

7. The Chariot
Triumph over financial difficulties, rivals and above all, over illness. Thus an indication of success in many areas.
Reversed: Ill health, undeserved success, restlessness.

8. Justice
Balance, legality, pedantry. Accountability for one's actions.
Reversed: Inequality, injustice. Merciful attitude to others.

9. Hermit
Meditation, prudence, receiving higher guidance. Thus a meeting with a wise counsellor who should be heeded.
Reversed: Immaturity, refusal to accept good advice.

10. Wheel of Fortune
Change, alteration — the endless highs and lows of life. Thus, unexpected change of fortune, sudden success.
Reversed: Failure and setbacks, demanding perseverance.

11. Strength
Courage, force of character, spiritual power triumphant over carnality. Thus the ability to overcome adversity, and hence any ill fortune shown in adjacent cards is modified.
Reversed: Materialism, lack of moral strength.

12. Hanged Man
To the spiritual — spiritual advancement. To the unaware — possible ill fortune. A pause in life, a withdrawal to develop inwardly. Thus, intuition, spirituality.
Reversed: Egotism, arrogance, false spirituality.

13. Death
Change, an ending — followed by a new beginning, perhaps in consciousness. Calm after a storm, reward after travail. But also, self-destructive fear.
Reversed: Inertia, stagnation. Revolution, perhaps assassination.

14. Temperance
Harmony with others, adaptation, successful timing.
Reversed: Quarrels, conflict of interests, separation.

15. Devil
Temptation, choice. Sometimes could

be inhumanity, carnality, illness.
Reversed: Dawn of spirituality and humility. Indecision.

16. Tower
Also known as the House of God. Catastrophe, undeserved disaster. Life style and ideas upset, permitting new enlightenment, but present material ambitions are likely to be thwarted.
Reversed: Oppression, perhaps false imprisonment. But through misfortune, freedom of body or spirit is gained.

17. Star
Hope, inspiration. Happiness-possibly fleeting. Spirituality glimpsed. Good health.
Reversed: Pessimism, obstinacy, gloom. Ill health.

18. Moon
Deception, secret enemies, unforeseen danger. Love misdirected or a loved one threatened. Intuitive powers increased.
Reversed: Practicality, avoidance of risk — but peace after storm.

19. Sun
Ambitions attained, material success, happy marriage, contentment — though none of these without proper labour.
Reversed: Plans unsettled. Loss, perhaps of job. Marriage problems.

20. Judgement
Awakening, new awareness. Strong influence of Fate. Spiritual union with the Absolute is near.
Reversed: Separation, disillusionment, loss of worldly goods.

21. World
Reward, success, fulfilment — not always in the way expected. State of cosmic consciousness and spiritual liberation.
Reversed: Fear of change, cramping of vision, success elusive.

The Minor Arcana

There are fifty-six cards in the Minor Arcana. They are divided into four suits: Cups, Swords, Pentacles and Wands (or Rods). These are the equivalents of Hearts, Spades. Diamonds and Clubs. There are fifty-six because each suit has an extra card, having four court cards instead of three: King, Queen, Knight and Knave.

The meanings of the suits

It is useful to remember that the suits have a significance of their own, and that a preponderance of one over the others slants the whole interpretation.
Cups Love, generosity, goodness.
Swords Disagreement, quarrels, strife.
Pentacles Intrigue. plots, politics.
Wands Change, travel, opportunity.
Upright or reversed, each of these fifty-six cards has a divinatory meaning and can alter the information which the Tarot pack gives us. But the main significance always lies in the Major Arcana and in the evocative and almost frightening power of the figures it portrays. The Minor Arcana can do no more than modify the broad outlines of the analyses and forecasts these stronger figures give. It tells of people's abilities and manoeuvres while they are protected or threatened by the greater forces which the Major Arcana represents.

Of course, anyone who wants to practice Taromancy seriously will have to learn the significance of, say, the Six of Pentacles as carefully as that of the High Priest or the Chariot, for its evidence may prove vital in the end.

The appeal of Tarot

It is clear that the Tarot pack can reach down to deep levels of the subconscious mind. Some people, when they see you produce a deck of these cards and proceed to lay them out, will, despite themselves, feel the tiny shiver of apprehension, of delight mixed with fear, which most of us experience when faced by the unknown, the uncanny, or the supernatural.

If you have learned to master the complexities of reading the Tarot pack, you have one certain way of stirring people's curiosity and holding their interest which you will have undoubtedly earned. For, besides knowing the meanings of each of the seventy-eight

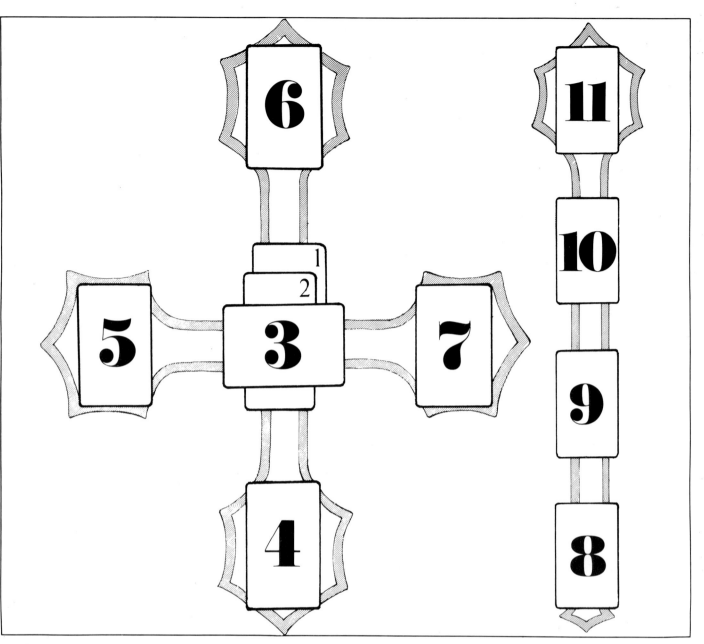

cards, the reading calls for a high level of intuition, plus the intelligence to combine the individual meanings with the promptings of intuition into one coherent interpretation. If you do achieve this mastery, there is no question that you and your friends will have a new pastime — and perhaps something more.

Lay-out of the Tarot cards

First, as in simple Cartomancy, choose a 'client' card. How, or even whether, you use it, will vary from one lay-out to another. The subject should then shuffle the cards. If you do it yourself, it helps if, before cutting the pack, the client lays a hand on it. Ask the client to concentrate on the questions to be asked.

Using the left hand, the client then cuts the pack into three piles, setting each pile down to the left of the one

before. Pick up the first of the piles laid down, also with your left hand, and begin laying out the cards in the pattern you have chosen. There are dozens of these, as one might expect after so many centuries of practice. Here are two of the most common:

Celtic cross
Place the 'client' card in the centre of the table. Now, in sequence and face up, lay out ten cards as follows:
Covering Card placed over the 'client' card. This gives the influence at work around the client in question.
Crossing Card laid sideways across the 'client' and Covering cards (though read as if upright). This shows what the opposing forces are. Note that if the Covering card is unfavourable, these opposing forces may be good.
Beneath Laid directly below the central cards, to form the first arm of a cross. This points to a past experience

relevant to the matter in hand.
Behind Laid to the left of the central cards, to form the second arm of the cross. This shows an influence just passing.
Crowning The upper arm of the cross — a possible future event.
Before The right-hand arm of the cross. This points to events in the very near future.
Now to the right of the cross, four cards are laid in a vertical row, starting from the bottom:
Fears The bottom card. This reveals the outcome of which the client is most afraid.
Environment Second from bottom. This card sums up the opinions of family and friends on the matter.
Hopes What does the client hope will happen?
Outcome The top card, and the last. This includes in summary the message of all the other cards, as well as

indicating what the outcome will be. If the last card proves to be impossible to interpret, or too vague, the best thing is to start again, this time placing it in the centre instead of the 'client' card. And in this as in all other cases, if there is still no satisfactory message, do not persevere. Put the cards away, for they have spoken — although only to say that they will not speak.

Tree of Life

This spread uses all 78 cards for a major 'life' reading. The first card is the central row or column; card 2 goes to the right, card 3 to the left. Then card 4 goes below 2, 5 goes below 3, and 6 goes below 1. Card 7 goes below 4, 8 below 5, 9 well below 6. Finally card 10 goes below 9, as it were on the trunk

of the tree. Then the other cards are dealt out in order on top until in each place there is a stack of seven cards The remaining eight are set aside.

In the interpretation of this layout, the cards of each stack refer to different aspects of life. The topmost stack contains cards referring to spirituality; 2 concerns creativity and initiative stack 3 relates to life's burdens. (2 and 3 are called the 'father' and 'mother' cards.) 4 can refer to virtues, but also to financial gain; stack 5 concerns strife and conquest; 6, health; but also fame; 7, love; 8, the arts, sciences and other skills; 9 concerns imagination, or health if that is not given to 6; and 10, on the tree trunk, is the home and sometimes corresponds to the physical body. The extra cards represent parts of the tree that are yet to come.

The ancient I Ching

The Book of Changes, which is I Ching in Chinese, is very old. Confucius and Lao Tse, founders of the two great streams of Chinese philosophy, turned to it for inspiration and information. It was regarded with such awe that in 213 BC, when the Emperor Ch'in Shih Huang Ti ordered a wholesale burning of books, it was one of the few which escaped. Its poetic teachings and symbolic commands, rich in metaphor, have had a great influence on the literature of China. Its intriguingly imprecise prophecies about the future were, until very recently, constantly referred to by the Chinese people, and those experienced in the interpretation of the I Ching were to be found in every village, almost in every street.

The philosophy

It is hard to say whether the I Ching reflected an already existing body of Chinese thought, or whether Chinese philosophy has been influenced by it to such an extent that it has almost derived from it. Certainly it is concerned with the duality of Yin and Yang, which is, very roughly, the opposition of the male — Yin — and the female — Yang — principles. Yin and Yang also stands for the tension between light and dark, the firm and the yielding, the sky and the earth. What is important for consideration of the Book of Changes is that such a state of universal tension means that the world is not static or inert. The ancient Chinese thinkers always rejected the notion of a motionless universe. They considered that events on this earth only mirrored the real events, which occured in a very different sphere, out of reach of all but a handful of the most highly developed human beings. So, what the I Ching offers is information about a world in flux — as its name implies, it is concerned with changes, with the driving forces which constantly modify life.

Since the book is concerned with action, rather than with a static picture of an unalterable state, it is also concerned with morality, with ideas of right and wrong. These are dealt with in the Judgements which accompany the pre-

The traditional Chinese way to cast hexagrams was with yarrow sticks.

dictions. They give the I Ching a dimension which no other method of scanning the future has. It not only predicts courses of action, it also gives some indication of whether their outcome will be beneficial or harmful. Consequently, people who consult the I Ching have an element of choice in their actions.

The role of fate

Underlying the morality of the I Ching is a belief in the prime importance of Fate. Changes happen all the time and everywhere, and this perpetual dynamic process depends upon the operation of Fate. The Chinese believed that God and Creation must get their energy from the workings of Fate. But these workings may be influenced and changed if anyone can put himself, as it were, in the place of a god and survey the future. The oracle in the I Ching allows that to be done. It does so by using the totality of every event, by treating nothing that occurs as being without meaning. Fate, or the mysterious supernatural forces through which it works, are everywhere and unceasingly active. The problem is to understand what their activity means.

Using the I Ching

First you need the book itself. This is freely available both in hardback and in paperback editions. Next you need either three coins or yarrow sticks. The latter are available from Chinese or fortune-telling shops. (Or you could, of course, find them growing wild and dry them yourself.) The book gives clear instructions on how to proceed from there — how to toss the coins or select the yarrow sticks, arrive at a hexagram and interpret it — to obtain a full reading.

The hexagrams

Of the two ways in which the I Ching may be consulted the first, using sticks, is rather complex and the other, using coins, is much simpler. Both methods, however, permit you to pick out the particular oracular statement which answers your question. Basically, these statements are an arrangement of six complete or broken lines,

forming a Hexagram.

In time past, it was believed that the oracle worked with the utmost simplicity, so that a complete line meant 'Yes', a broken one 'No'. But this came to seem inadequate, and the unbroken and the broken lines were joined in four combinations, and a third line was added to them. This gave the possibility of eight arrangements, or trigrams, to each of which a particular meaning was given. These symbols were again combined, and the arrangements changed from three to six lines. This achieved two results: each symbol became far richer in meaning, and the number of symbols was at once increased from eight to sixty-four. The I Ching had, in its essence, been created.

Method of consultation

The hexagram which answers a particular question is built up line by line.

The yarrow sticks
The Chinese sages used yarrow sticks and a complicated formula to arrive at the hexagram they wanted. This is described in detail in the book.

Coins
The alternative method, using coins, is much more practical today. In ancient times, the Chinese themselves used brass coins with a hollow in the middle, but ordinary coins will do as well. Three of these are used, with heads being given the value of three, tails that of two.

The three coins are tossed and the value they make together, once they come to rest, will be six, seven, eight or nine. The first two stand for broken lines, the last two for unbroken lines. Thus, each throw of the coins gives a line of one sort or the other and when you have thrown six times, you will have the hexagram you need. In the key with which each copy of the Book of Changes is provided you now look up the hexagram's number, and in this way find the page which tells you its meaning.

Interpretation

At this point, however, things become both more complicated and more interesting.

	Name	Attribute	Image	Family Relationship
☰	Chi'en the Creative	strong	heaven	father
☷	K'un the Receptive	devoted, yielding	earth	mother
☳	Chên the Arousing	inciting movement	thunder	first son
☵	K'an the Abysmal	dangerous	water	second son
☶	Kên Keeping Still	resting	mountain	third son
☴	Sun the Gentle	penetrating	wind, wood	first daughter
☲	Li the Clinging	light–giving	fire	second daughter
☱	Tui the Joyous	joyful	lake	third daughter

Upper Trigram ► Lower Trigram ▼	Ch'ien ☰	Chên ☳	K'an ☵	Kên ☶	K'un ☷	Sun ☴	Li ☲	Tui ☱
Ch'ien ☰	1	4	5	26	11	9	14	43
Chên ☳	25	51	3	27	24	42	21	17
K'an ☵	6	40	29	4	7	59	64	47
Kên ☶	33	62	39	52	15	53	56	31
K'un ☷	12	16	8	23	2	20	35	45
Sun ☴	44	32	48	18	46	57	50	28
Li ☲	13	55	63	22	36	37	30	49
Tui ☱	10	54	60	41	19	61	38	58

Key to the construction of the hexagrams

119

The world to which the hexagram's advice seems to apply, and the language in which it is given, make much of what is written in the I Ching strange at first glance. It is like trying to make sense of a fragment of poetry which has been translated from another language and another time. You will read of kings and princes, of lakes and mountains, of wanderers and sages, and wonder whether this can really apply to you. Sometimes. the very vagueness of the text allows it to have what seems to be a suitable meaning. It is possible to read into the words more than they actually hold. At other times, however, the advice can be very explicit.

Imagine that you are going to meet a man of slightly doubtful commercial reputation. You decide to ask of the I Ching whether he is to be trusted. The coins give Hexagram 13, 'Fellowship with Men'. Under the heading 'Judgement', are the following words:
'Fellowship with men in the open
Success
It furthers one to cross the great water
The perseverance of the superior man furthers'

The interpretation of this tells you, among other things, 'It is not the private interests of the individual that create lasting fellowship among men, but rather the goals of humanity. That is why it is said that fellowship with men in the open succeeds. If unity of this kind prevails, even difficult and dangerous tasks, such as crossing the great water, can be accomplished'.

Selection of lines

At this stage, another element enters the interpretation. Each line of the hexagram has a meaning, but you select only those lines for which you have thrown coins totalling either nine or six — in other words, all heads or all tails. These are the strong yang or yin lines and modify the general meaning of the oracle. When the coins total seven or eight, the lines have no individual meaning, but only help to build the hexagram. With a nine in the third line (reading, as one must, from the bottom up) this gives a new text:
'He hides weapons in the thicket
He climbs the high hill in front of it
For three years he does not rise up'
The interpretation of this (again in

Bottom left: In this engraving of a scene set in ancient China, yarrow sticks are being used. Above right: coins are a substitute for yarrow sticks in the casting of the hexagrams.

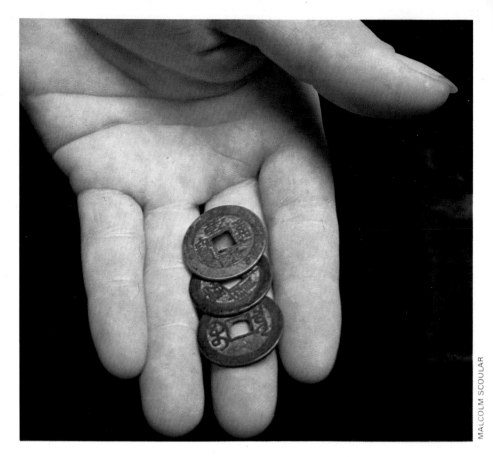

MALCOLM SCOULAR

part) is 'Obstacles standing in the way of fellowship with others are shown here. One has mental reservations for one's own part and seeks to take one's opponent by surprise. This very fact makes one mistrustful . . The result is that one departs further and further from true fellowship.'

All this seems to suggest that suspicions about the man you are to meet are unworthy and liable to do more harm than good. By not trusting him you will bring about the very situation which you fear. But the interpretation still needs one more phase.

Line reversal

When a strong yin or yang line, a line with the value nine or six, appears in a hexagram it has to be reversed, thus making a new hexagram which must in its turn be interpreted. Thus, the yang line, the unbroken line third from the bottom, was now changed to a broken yin line, and that gives Hexagram 25, Innocence (The Unexpected). 'Innocence. Supreme success.
Perseverance furthers.
If someone is not as he should be,
He has misfortune,
And it does not further him
To undertake anything.'
That is the Judgement, and its interpretation begins 'Man has received from heaven a nature innately good, to guide him in all his movements. By

devotion to this divine spirit within himself, he attains an unsullied innocence that leads him to do right with instinctive sureness and without any ulterior thought of reward and personal advantage.' So it would appear, finally, that as long as you are honest in your intentions and do not allow suspicion of this person to cloud your attitudes, everything will go very well. The I Ching is a very seductive oracle. The very fact that it is not easy to grasp, that one has to work to make its messages clear, also makes it attractive.

However as the detailed example of interpretation shows, it can be practical, and it does seem to address itself to the problems raised. Of course, this is partly because the language of the I Ching is vague enough to apply to almost anything. Yet there are sixty-three other hexagrams which the coins might have chosen, many of which are much less well-adapted to answer a question dealing with suspicions about another person. Perhaps the ancient Chinese knew a thing or two about what makes coins fall in particular sequences, or why yarrow sticks should make patterns which are not really random at all. In any case, they have left us the I Ching, and whatever else its value may be, it certainly makes an unusual and absorbing game for agile-minded people who have an imaginative love of words.